Excused ABSENCE

D1167145

CruXpress
books that matter

ABSENCE

SHOULD CHRISTIAN KIDS LEAVE PUBLIC SCHOOLS?

Douglas Wilson

CruXpress
books that matter

MISSION VIEJO, CALIFORNIA

Excused Absence: Should Christian Kids Leave Public Schools?

Published by
Crux Press, Inc.
28715 Los Alisos Blvd., #7-418
Mission Viejo, California 92692
800.707.CRUX
www.cruxpress.com

Cover design by Dwayne Cogdill, Cognition Design

Printed in the United States of America

Unless otherwise indicated, Scripture quotations are from the New King James Version, ©1979, 1980, 1982 by Thomas Nelson, Inc., Publishers, Nashville, Tennessee. Scripture quotations designated KJV are from the King James Version.

ISBN 0-9702245-1-6

For Jemima Donne

ACKNOWLEDGMENTS

Many thanks to David Hagopian for his friendship, editing, commitment, and humor. I also thank Crux Press for giving me this opportunity, as well as Joette Whims and Lynn Copeland for their editorial assistance, and Terri Oesterreich for her typesetting.

CONTENTS

FOREWORD

U.S. senators, eat your hearts out! You'd salivate at the opportunity to grill Doug Wilson upon the occasion of his nomination to be Secretary of Education. But that won't happen, because Doug is terrific at producing the zingers that make him unappointable.

Just imagine what a Ted Kennedy would do with Doug's observation that "we find a *jihad* against racism, pollution, or global warming in the government schools at one moment, then seconds later, we find the same absolutist zealots insisting that there is no such thing as absolute good or evil when it comes to homosexuality or other 'alternative lifestyles.'"

Doug produces light as well as heat. Here's a point every Christian needs to understand: "When God is excluded from the classroom, we are not merely remaining silent about God. We are teaching children that they may safely disregard Him. Whether or not God exists, the lesson goes, His existence is irrelevant to what we are doing here. So when God is omitted, we are not silent about Him; rather, we are teaching the children in the most convincing way possible that God is irrelevant. They can safely omit Him when it is convenient to do so."

I do think Doug overdoes it at times. For example, regarding Christians teaching at government schools, he writes, "Put simply, the teacher can make a difference or not. If he makes a difference, his case will probably appear before the Supreme

Court. If he is not making a difference, then why not go where he can?" That is put too simply: teachers make a difference in many different ways, some legally actionable, some not. Doug would want readers of this book to think through his points themselves and object at times.

Still, *Excused Absence* is stimulating reading, and parents— "particularly those fathers who do the opposite of what the Bible commands and leave educational decisions to their wives"— need to think through its counsel. Doug does not shy from uncomfortable truths. He points out, for instance, that Protestants during the nineteenth century lorded it over Catholics, and writes that "part of our problem today" having a foreign worldview imposed on us "is that we did not have a problem when we were doing it to others."

It's time to stop the new imposition: We should repent for past sins and try, with God's grace, not to start a new sequence of wrongs. Doug Wilson teaches us to think through biblical ways of starting anew.

MARVIN OLASKY
Senior fellow, Acton Institute,
and editor, *World*

1
THE TRUE
STARTING POINT

* *"I advise no one to place his child where the Scriptures do not reign
paramount. Every institution in which men are not increasingly
occupied with the Word of God must become corrupt . . .
I am much afraid that schools will prove to be the great gates of hell
unless they diligently labor in explaining the Holy Scriptures,
engraving them in the hearts of youth."*
—MARTIN LUTHER

When it comes to government schools, we are all too familiar
with some of the recent battlegrounds. What do we do about
drug deals and guns? What about Outcome-Based Education?
Should we teach right from wrong? Can we pray in the classroom? Should creationism be taught? Add to this list another
item—a question recently asked by two legal scholars: Can we
teach sexual abstinence in government schools without somehow violating the separation between church and state?

When confronted with new issues like this abstinence
argument, Christians usually respond by trying to reform government schools in some fashion—writing letters to the editor,
seeking the floor at the next school board meeting, or running
for a vacancy on the PTA. Each of these responses, however,
misses the point that "reforming" government schools will
never solve their fundamental problem: they are based on institutional agnosticism, if not outright hostility to the Christian
faith. In light of this undeniable reality, Christian parents really

face one of two choices: either educate their children with Christ or educate them against Him. No other alternatives exist. In the end, Christian parents are called by God to educate their children not only about abstinence, but also about everything else under the sun He created. The alternative to the unhealthy secular fare regularly served up to our children today is not a dash of religious seasoning, but a whole new recipe.

That's where this book comes in. It aims to persuade Christian parents to act wisely in their children's education by giving them the kind of education the Bible requires: a distinctively Christian education, which their children cannot receive at government schools.

To establish this point, we will not cite studies on the general state of government education in our country, because we are awash in such studies. In fact, the only thing we learn from these studies is that they don't make any difference—just like our schools. If they were what we really needed, all our educational problems would have been solved long ago.

Is and Ought

The issue is not statistics, but morality. The issue ultimately is not what the situation is but what we should do as parents. Consequently, this book will focus on the reasons Christian children need to receive a distinctively Christian education, either in a traditional Christian school setting or at home. And I will be blunt in the process. The unbelieving state of government schools and the covenant responsibilities of Christian parents combine to create a need for some straight talk and concerted action.

The obligation of Christians to provide a Christian education for their children is one that existed in Scripture long before prayer and the Ten Commandments were driven out of government schools. It existed long before atheistic educators like Horace Mann or John Dewey ever had an unbelieving thought in their heads. Accordingly, we cannot find the foundation for our renewed obedience merely by tracing the historical development of our disobedience. In other words, our educational obligations do not come into existence through any reaction to the dismal state of government schools. Of course, when the dismal state of those schools causes some parents to reconsider their biblical responsibilities, we rejoice. But we all would do well to remember that there was a time in our history when the government schools were much less offensive but still just as wrong in principle.

We must define the basic biblical issues clearly, then apply them to our contemporary situation. We must seek to understand the biblical principles, then act from those principles. Reaction is no basis for renewal in education. Simply pulling away is very different from repentance. Repentance is radical, going to the root of the problem. Reaction is superficial and runs away from drug deals, guns, Outcome-Based Education, outlawed prayer, evolution, sex education, and all the rest, without ever really understanding why these things are upon us. When your basement is flooding, the first thing to find is the main valve, not a bucket and sponge. Because government education is failing, we need to get to the source, and avoid hiding the symptoms.

Cherished Beliefs

Education is the process of taking a culture's values, assumptions, traditions, and beliefs, then transmitting them from one generation to the next. Because our culture is in crisis, we should not be surprised that the process of education also is in crisis. We have established a vast machinery for educating our children—compulsory education laws to require attendance for many years, significant tax burdens on property owners to pay for it all, and politicians who promise to support this ganglion of problems. We have built an immense mechanism to pass on our cherished beliefs to our children, but, much to our chagrin, we have now come to discover that we no longer have any cherished beliefs.

Actually, we do have one cherished belief left—that our government schools exist "for the kids," and that a vote for school levies is necessarily a vote "for the kids." Anyone who differs with this belief, we are told, must be hostile to kids. This cherished belief remains with us largely through inertia. We keep doing what we have done because we do not know what else to do, and all we have left is the hollow rhetoric of a previous era. ‒ As we have seen in many cultures—such as the pragmatic picture of Cicero in ancient Rome—functional idolatry usually outlasts a true belief in the gods. Cynicism about the deities may abound, but for the sake of cultural cohesion and continuity, the sacrifices continue. This inertia is where we are today.

Selling Out

We cannot dispute that modern secular education is an outdated idol. Horace Mann, who lived from 1796 to 1858, can safely be considered the father of government schools in the United States. He once reflected his trust in "his savior" when he said that education is our only political safety. Outside of this ark, he thought, all is deluge. But despite the best efforts of our best pedagogues, this ark continues to sink. Contrary to the instructions given, we did not build it from gopher wood, thinking instead to try the bricks of atheistic science and the cinder blocks of godless rationalism. Some things just don't float as well.

H. G. Wells echoed this understanding of the basic human dilemma when he said that our history was turning into a race between education and catastrophe. Those who have grave doubts about the efficacy of our educational system know that catastrophe is really and permanently bad. They have severe doubts about our educational system, but no doubts at all about the "catastrophe." Because they believe that education and catastrophe are the only choices on the menu, they continue to place their orders by clinging to long-discredited nostrums. What is the alternative?

Tragically, many Christian parents are entangled in this disastrous reasoning and have come to share several idolatrous assumptions of their unbelieving neighbors. On any given day from September to June, an agnostic family, a Muslim family, an atheist family, a Buddhist family, and a Christian family all see to it that their children clamber onto the very same yellow school bus and get shuttled off to learn about the world God made, or the world that evolved, or whatever works.

We have proven to be very naive about the ways education can be utilized. As Joseph Stalin put it, ‒"Education is a weapon, whose effects depend on who holds it in his hands and at whom it is aimed."-

Under our current circumstances, naiveté is disobedience and therefore dangerous. Christian parents who seek to educate their children in the government school system allow their children to be instructed according to the tenets of another religion. - The problem is even worse because the very existence of our government school system depends upon an ongoing willingness of Christian parents to surrender their children. The secular state has made a "free" education available, and all that we need to do is to turn our children over to be taught that God is irrelevant to all of life's pursuits. They learn that every subject of study can be competently addressed (or so the claim goes) without any reference to Him. For some reason, Christian parents go along with this reasoning. Why? -

A free education need not be a Christian education. Put another way, when we sold our kids, we got a good price for them.

What Lies Ahead

In the pages to follow, we will see that God calls Christian parents to think clearly about the education of their children. In order to understand our divine calling, we first must take a look at how we got government schools and where we find ourselves today (chapter 2). We also must acknowledge the root of the problem in our homes (chapter 3).

After painting this backdrop, we will discuss the six reasons Christian children need a distinctively Christian education. First, neutrality is impossible in any endeavor, much less in education. Christ is Lord of all, including the three cornerstones of all true Christian education: truth (chapter 4), beauty (chapter 5), and goodness (chapter 6).

Second, although government schools are built on the quicksand of pragmatism (the belief that truth is what works), government schools cannot really "work" because they ignore the context for all true education (chapter 7).

-Third, the Bible requires parents to educate their children in accordance with a biblical worldview from the time they get up until the time they go to sleep (chapter 8). -

◄Fourth, God calls us to train our children to love Him not only with all their heart, soul, and strength, but also with all their mind (chapter 9). ▬

Fifth, there is no such thing as a free lunch, but for too long Christian parents have believed that public education is free, when the "legal tender" paid is indeed tender—their very children (chapter 10).

Sixth, Christian parents disobey God at their peril and the peril of their children by offering them to the three false gods of all government education: pragmatism, pluralism, and relativism (chapter 11).

After presenting the biblical case for providing our children with a distinctively Christian education, we will discuss several common objections and answer them based on Scripture (chapter 12). Then we will turn our attention to what makes an education truly Christian (chapter 13). We also will look at pitfalls of both Christian schools and Christian homeschools (chapter 14), the missing ingredients of all government schools (chapter 15), and the need for covenant love and joy that only a true Christian education, by the grace of God, can produce (chapter 16). Finally, we will wrap up by reminding ourselves that-there can be no good thing apart from faith in the Lord who made and saved us, who promises to be our all in all (chapter 17).▬

You Gotta Believe

Throughout this book, we must keep in mind the biblical truth that we will explore in the last chapter: that faith without works is dead, and its corollary, that works without faith is rank legalism. We begin the Christian life by grace, and we end it by grace (Eph. 2:8–9). It is grace, grace, and more grace throughout. But we are God's workmanship, created for good works, which He prepared beforehand that we should walk in them (Eph. 2:10). Therefore, it is high time to walk in those good works regarding our children.

We also must understand two fundamentals of the faith. The first is the antithesis or contrast between belief and unbelief that pervades all reality. The second is the biblical definition of the good life. We must master the antithesis so that we do not accept spurious forms of education for our children. And we must understand the good life so that we know what and how we are to teach. We study the antithesis so that we might know what to avoid, and we study the good life so that we know what to provide. Along the way, we must discover that genuine Christian education is not optional. It is a biblical mandate.

So we turn now to how we got where we find ourselves today—how we ended up with government schools at war with God.

2
HOW WE GOT HERE

✶ *"The United States system of national popular education will be the most efficient and wide instrument for the propagation of Atheism which the world has ever seen."*
—A. A. HODGE   ✗

The American character is a fascinating study, and we cannot understand it apart from the process of education that we have adopted. We can trace the degeneration of the American character by looking at the change in our education from Christian education to a secular agenda. ⁻

The Older Order

When our colonies were first established, we were a European people, particularly characterized by the flavor of the British Isles with an overwhelming Scottish and Scotch-Irish influence. Compared to the rest of Europe, the British Isles had a longer and more deeply entrenched tradition of liberty under law. We inherited this tradition from the very first and exhibited this character very clearly. In the middle colonies and in the South, this influence was greatest from Scottish and Scotch-Irish immigrants. In the early eighteenth century, these Calvinistic Presbyterians came to the colonies by the hundreds of thousands. They brought the mentality of the older order. When the common schools were first established on a widespread basis, their model was a "new and scientific" import from Prussia.

"Progressive" education—education that was more modern and scientific—already had deep roots on the Continent, going back to the time of an educational reformer named Jan Amos Comenius, who was born in 1592. He became a bishop in the Union of Bohemian Brethren, which was the most biblical branch of the Moravians. He was a man of exemplary personal piety, but this piety was unfortunately employed in the propagation of a host of progressive and utopian ideas in education. These ideas afflict us to this day. To use Jean-Marc Berthoud's memorable summary, Comenius was the "forerunner of all the most lethal errors which we associate with the totalitarian utopias and revolutionary messianic political orders which have ravaged the modern world."

As the population of Europe grew, the thoughts of more and more intellectuals turned to progressive education as an important element of social engineering. Of course, the same ideological tendencies were at work in the British Isles, but with greater conflict. Many of those most hostile to the rising tide of humanistic rationalism decided to come to our shores.

Two Great Impulses

Up through the eighteenth century, our nation was a part of the older order of Christendom. But by the beginning of the nineteenth century, this old order began to collapse.

This collapse of the old orthodoxies in America stemmed from two great impulses. The first was simply the *force of gravity*. The "natural man," no matter where or when he lives, does not love the doctrines of grace, and he will slip the leash first chance he gets. The Christian worldview does not flatter man, and man in his rebellion loves to be flattered. Thus, when a Christian culture comes to the point where a large number of people are unregenerate, a collision is inevitable. A Christian ethic is generally held by that culture through inertia, but those who do not love God chafe under its restrictions, particularly sexual restrictions. The stage, therefore, is set for a revolt. This impulse is why we constantly need to preach the gospel powerfully, especially in ostensibly Christian nations.

But coupled with this impulse was a second impulse: *a rising individualism and sense of self-reliance,* which came from living on the frontier. The myth of American "rugged individualism" began to develop at this time and radically redefined the nature of the Christian faith. Instead of taking great satisfaction from living in the midst of the church as a covenant community, the frontier heroes were "magnificent" in their isolation. As one frontiersman put it, when he got to "fightin' b'ar," he felt mighty numerous.

Humanism's Coup

We see both processes at work in the early part of the nineteenth century. In the North, the Second Great Awakening, led by men like Charles Finney, redirected evangelical zeal in a very man-centered direction. The focus on methodology reigned supreme. Religious enthusiasm remained only to obscure the departure of genuine Christian faith.

Finney denied cardinal doctrines of the Christian faith such as the substitutionary atonement of Christ. But he obscured this denial through his enthusiastic promotion of revivals. To this day, many define the term *evangelical* apart from confessional doctrinal content and in terms of intensity of a religious encounter with Jesus, whoever the zealot thinks Jesus is. In Finney's hands, a revival was nothing more than the right manipulation of certain techniques conducive to "saving souls."

It was through Finney that humanism became established in evangelical circles, and *because of Finney,* many evangelicals are unable to recognize the antithesis between the humanism of government schools and what they hear in their pulpits. Evangelicals cannot see the antithesis between the two because there is no fundamental difference between secular humanism and religious humanism tricked out with a few Christian decorations.

Around the same time as Finney, the unbelief of humanistic Unitarianism—the heretical denial of the Trinity and other truths of orthodox Christianity in favor of doctrines such as the perfectibility of mankind and self-improvement—was rampant among New England's intellectual elite. Harvard was captured by the Unitarians in 1805, but the response of the evangelicals was unfortunately just as humanistic as the overt liberalism they battled. The revivals were just as man-centered as the unbelief that had captured the intellectual centers. New evangelical and Unitarian leaders were therefore able to agree on one thing: The old historic Protestant orthodoxy had to go. That orthodoxy was dismissed under the nickname of *Calvinism*, but that nickname represented the mainstream Protestant conviction from the Reformation down to the turn of the nineteenth century. Prior to this great apostasy, Christians in this country were overwhelmingly "Calvinistic"—Presbyterian, Congregational, and Baptist.

Arising on the political front at this time was Jacksonian democracy, a self-conscious rejection of the older aristocratic order. That older order, as mentioned before, was Christian, and the new order, despite loud claims of faith in God, was actually driven by faith in a new god, *demos*—the people.

As we consider the rise of government education, we have to remember that these things never happen suddenly as if someone turned the lights off. We are dealing with millions of people and a culture in transition. We can find many elements of the old and new existing side by side. Some representatives of the older order are still alive today, and advocates of modernity could be found earlier than this turning point. Nevertheless, this period of rising humanism, revivalism, rationalism, and democratism created the climate in which our government school movement came into being.

The "Common Schools"

Having set this stage, we must back up for a moment and consider the "common schools" of New England, which were a feature of colonial life almost from the beginning. These common schools, although not numerous, were supported through taxes, and thus, were public schools. Therefore, we can distinguish *tax-supported education* from what we have now, which is tax-supported *pluralistic* education. The former had been found in various forms in the Reformed countries of Europe. John Knox and Martin Luther had both been involved in establishing common schools. The New England Puritans followed them in this enterprise, and thus unwittingly set the stage for the horrific takeover of these schools. But the religious climate of New England had been homogenous with established state churches existing into the early nineteenth century. Put another way, the first government schools in America were *Christian* schools.

Thus, society-wide insistence on the education of other people's children existed *before* the rise of secularism. It was not necessarily before the rise of some "progressive" thinking about education. (Remember the influence of earlier progressives like Comenius.) But that thinking, while pernicious, had not yet borne its bitter fruit in America.

This call for general education, although somewhat authoritarian, was manifested in the midst of a homogenous culture where the thought of our current smorgasbord approach to education would have been appalling. Though the New England fathers were unwise to form tax-supported schools, they were not guilty of the folly of pluralism. Their error was genuine, but compared to ours, it was trivial. These schools were few in number, and they were localized in New England where the Puritans had always tended to a little "godly" bossiness. So tax-funded schools are a bad idea, but they pale in comparison to tax-supported centers for the propagation of pluralistic agnosticism.

As R. L. Dabney clearly pointed out, the New England Puritans agreed to public schools only because there was at that time no separation between church and state as we have today, and the state was committed by law to teaching in the light of the Reformed faith. As Dabney put it:

> If Knox had seen a severance of Church and State (which he would have denounced as wicked and pagan) leading to a secular education, which trained the intellect without the conscience or heart, his heroic tongue would have given no uncertain sound.

In the middle colonies and in the South, a broader and more consistent Reformed theology prevailed and did not result in any government schools. So taking one thing with another, this climate, from the founding of the colonies down to the beginning of the nineteenth century, was a predominantly Christian vision of education.

Turning South

That initial vision was supplanted beginning in the nineteenth century, even though many of the Christian trappings remained in place down through the twentieth century. In the nineteenth century, one of the fathers of modern atheistic American education arrived on the scene—Horace Mann. Although he had been brought up in the Calvinistic faith, he came to hate that faith with passion. Mann was a convinced Unitarian and mirrored the apostasy of virtually the entire New England intellectual elite. Under the influence of Mann, the "common schools" began to spread in New England and areas affected by New England.

The New England intelligentsia did not make any progress in the South where the intellectual leadership was still orthodox and Christian. The South had government schools imposed on her later in the aftermath of the War Between the States. Resistance to the spreading common schools was solid in the South because the Second Great Awakening had been far more doctrinally sound than in New England and had not led to the same problems as were visible in the North. In fact, the general apostasy of the North was one of the factors in the building tension that ultimately led to civil war. The government schools in the South were established as part of a larger cultural conquest, which occurred as a result of a lot of bloodshed.

An interesting tension developed. The intellectual movement behind the spreading government schools consisted almost exclusively of unbelievers. But because the society was still sufficiently decentralized, each local school was run by school boards, which were mostly evangelical and Christian. The pagans built the machinery, and the Christians volunteered to run it at the local level. And the memory of this local control explains why so many Christians today still accept the notion that the government schools are somehow "our" schools.

Doing Unto Others

When these schools were first established, the Roman Catholics felt that the government schools were Protestant and were not *their* schools. Protestant Bibles were used; Protestant prayers were said; Protestant catechisms were recited. The Roman Catholic parochial school system grew out of this development. The Catholics didn't necessarily see the approaching secularism in the classroom before the Protestants did; they simply objected to Protestantism in the classroom. So the Catholic parochial school system was formed because of the conviction (accurate enough at the time) that the government school system was basically the school system for Protestants.

At this time, the United States had an *informal* established religion—evangelical Protestantism. As an established religion, it enjoyed support from taxpayers. But the taxpayers included increasing numbers of people who were not evangelical Protestants. The great wave of immigration in the nineteenth century, for example, brought in thousands upon thousands of Irish Catholics. When they arrived, they found themselves being taxed to support a school system that propagated a worldview foreign to theirs.

Part of our problem today—having a foreign worldview imposed on *us*—is that we did *not* have a problem when we were doing it to *others*. Now that *others* are doing it to *us*, we yell like we really hate injustice. But what goes around comes around. Christian parents need to understand the *principles* involved, especially whose ox is being gored. What Catholics opposed when Protestants were behind the wheel, Protestants now oppose when secularists are behind the wheel. Because of this fact, we do not have the moral authority to object. Without repentance, we will never have that moral authority.

The Final Takeover

Protestants were content with the informal establishment of their religion and were comfortable with the idea of government schools as friendly to them. They thought this state of affairs would last forever all by itself, untended and unguarded. But as the twentieth century unfolded, modernity proved itself to be more and more overtly hostile. Christians had been content with the removal of the substance of the Christian faith, but they had been allowed, for a time, to keep the trappings. But because unbelief hates even the *name* of the Lord Jesus Christ, the final takeover eventually began.

Some saw it coming. Long before the overt secularization of government education, Dabney prophesied in the nineteenth century that it was just a matter of time. He said:

> Nearly all public men and preachers declare that the public schools are the glory of America. They are a finality, and in no event to be surrendered. We have seen that their complete secularization is logically inevitable. Christians must prepare themselves, then, for the following results: All prayers, catechisms, and Bibles will ultimately be driven out of the schools.

We read these words and wonder aloud to ourselves, "We used to have catechisms in the schools?" We remember when prayer was driven out in the sixties, but we do not realize that the government schools used to be Christian schools with far more Christian content than exists in many private Christian schools today. But even though they were Christian schools, they were unwisely established on a secular foundation. Those with wisdom saw that such an institution eventually had to have consistency between the foundation and the superstructure. They also saw that the secular foundation was going to prevail.

Ideas and Consequences

The secular foundation was bound to prevail because ideas have consequences, which work themselves out over time. The rapidity with which the vestiges of the once-dominant Christian faith have been thrown out of the government schools within the last generation does not represent a massive and recent assault by the forces of secularization. Rather, it indicates the patience of those forces. Secularists set the machinery of this particular takeover in place in the latter half of the last century, and they built the machine to operate slowly and imperceptibly.

The work has been done over the course of numerous generations. Just because we see the symbols of the old order tumbling rapidly, we should not conclude that everything was fine shortly before. The crash of a house may be spectacular and may seem very sudden, but no one was watching when the termites were quietly doing their work.

- American Christians were allowed to believe that their faith would be protected, even propagated, in the government schools and that their values would be respected. But this was all a lie, and the sooner we come to recognize that lie, the sooner we can come to grips with the problems we now face. -

And the problems we now face didn't just appear in the classroom. The root of these problems grows at home and branches out from there. We need to turn briefly and get to the root of the problem.

3
GETTING TO
THE ROOT

"Therefore it is apparent, that the ordinary appointed means
for the first actual grace, is parents' godly instruction
and education of their children."
—RICHARD BAXTER

Because sin is the great destroyer, we should not be surprised
that it lies behind the great abdication that established our government school system. But, as always, great sins come from
little ones, and the established school system would have been
impossible apart from countless acts of disobedience in the living room and around the dinner table.

Below the Surface of Garden-Variety Sins
While addressing common sins in the household, it would be
too easy to focus on those garden-variety sins everyone knows
and acknowledges to be sins, such as complaining and fighting.
But we must take a step or two back to address some of the problems that set up the temptations for these sins. Long ago,
Malachi prophesied:

> Behold, I will send you Elijah the prophet before the
> coming of the great and dreadful day of the LORD. And
> he will turn the hearts of the fathers to the children,
> and the hearts of the children to their fathers, lest I
> come and strike the earth with a curse (Mal. 4:5–6).

The New Testament teaches us that Malachi's prophecy was fulfilled in Christ. John the Baptist came before the Lord, and the point of John the Baptist's ministry (a ministry of *preparation*) was to turn the hearts of fathers and children to each other. Note also the alternative—a curse upon the earth. When fathers and mothers are honored and the atmosphere is spiritually healthy in the home, the result is blessing in the land. When the family breaks down, everything breaks down.

The Root Problem

But simply having traditional family values on paper does not prevent such breakdowns. How we educate and rear our children is a matter of central concern because millions of souls are at stake. Whatever the issue, we have to think biblically.

We often deal with sins only when they bear fruit at the branch's extremities. A lot of spiritual energy could be spared if we were willing to consider some of the root problems. So what are some of the root problems in the home?

Spiritual Neglect. The first root problem in the home is spiritual neglect; those who do not know the condition of their own souls are in no position to shepherd the souls of others. Our Lord pinpointed this problem in His parable of the sower: "Now the ones that fell among thorns are those who, when they have heard, go out and are choked with cares, riches, and pleasures of life, and bring no fruit to maturity" (Luke 8:14).

Parents, take care that you do not neglect the state of your own soul with "cares, riches, and pleasures of life." So how is it with you and God? *Busyness* is not holiness, even busyness in the work of ministry. We cannot be too busy to care for our souls and the souls of our children. It is our divine calling. And caring for the souls of our children necessarily involves how they are educated and what they are taught every minute of every day.

Defensive Isolationism. Another root problem is defensive isolationism. Paul tells us many things: "Wives, submit . . . Husbands, love . . . Children, obey . . . Fathers, do not provoke . . ." (Col. 3:18–21). The point is not the specific content of Paul's exhortations, but rather that in the context of this passage, he gives the commands to the church.

We live in community; we are not a club of isolated individuals. The fact that the church is a community means that we should be involved in one another's lives, which, in turn, means that we should be involved with one another's children.

Many parents falsely assume that they know their children better than anyone else in the church does. It would be more accurate to say that parents could know their children better if they studied the Word and their children with biblical wisdom. And if they did, then they would know that "faithful are the wounds of a friend, but the kisses of an enemy are deceitful" (Prov. 27:6).

Those who give their children a distinctively Christian education should do so because they do not want the sin of the world pumped into their children, but they also should be careful not to fall into the sin of isolationism, cutting themselves off from the church. The church may have a school, but the school is not the church. The home may be a school, but the home is not the church.

Ignorant Isolationism. Another great problem is ignorant isolationism. Just as sin seeks the darkness (John 3:19), it also seeks *lack of accountability*. But Paul is blunt in telling us that we dare not class ourselves or compare ourselves with those who isolate themselves: "But they, measuring themselves by themselves, and comparing themselves among themselves, are *not wise*" (2 Cor. 10:12).

Ignorant isolationism is a common problem among those who neglect the education of their children. Parents who would rather not be troubled to teach their children also would rather not be troubled by those reminding them that they don't. Consequently, problems that arise are often not identified until it is too late to do anything about it.

Presumption. Many Christian parents are blinded by presumption. Far from neglecting community, this sin relies entirely on "community." "All we have to do," these parents think, "is enroll our children in a good school, attend church, make sure that we hang around, and everything will turn out all right." *No, it won't.*

When parents do not exercise godly and wise oversight with their children, bad things regularly and *routinely* happen, regardless of the community in which the children live or the school they attend.

Dropping your kids off at Sunday school is no substitute for teaching them from the time they rise up until they go to bed (Deut. 6:4–9). God calls us as parents to train and educate our children all the time, and we cannot do it by proxy. The responsibility ultimately belongs to us. We will answer to Him for how, by His grace, we fulfill that responsibility.

Fads. Parents too often chase after spiritual fads. Paul, however, longs "that we should no longer be children, tossed to and fro and carried about with every wind of doctrine, by the trickery of men, in the cunning craftiness of deceitful plotting, but, speaking the truth in love, may grow up in all things into Him who is the head—Christ" (Eph. 4:14–15).

We may divide fads into two categories. On the one hand, some fads fit the description in Ephesians exactly and are destructive. All anti-biblical forms of legalism fit into this category. But we also should include those fads that consist of good things which could be fruitful and constructive *if approached with wisdom*, such as courtship, homeschools, Christian schools, etc. Stampedes never bring wisdom so we must always avoid the herd mentality.

Shortsightedness. Far too many parents struggle with shortsightedness. Bringing up children—training and educating them—is like pouring concrete. Time is a key element, and after that time has passed, the thing is *done.*

While God is gracious, most studies demonstrate that what a young person believes upon graduating from college will often be what he believes the rest of his life. Therefore, we need to redeem the time and use it wisely.

When you are dealing with the future, what is the foundation for your confidence? If it is anything other than the triune God of Scripture, you have no surety. He is our only confidence and hope in this life and the life to come.

Covenant Headship

At the root of many of the problems we have identified is the fact that modern fathers do not own up to the biblical doctrine of covenant connectedness. They do not understand that the family is a covenantal or "federal" entity. The Latin word for covenant is *foedus*, from which we get the word *federal*. We are thrown off by this terminology because our current "federal" government today is very *un*federal, *un*covenantal.

From a biblical viewpoint, however, marriages are covenants. This description is no less true of the fruit of those covenant unions. The family is not established by custom or by legislation. The family is established and defined by the Word of God alone. We have to turn to that Word to understand the responsibilities of Christian fathers.

> His sons would go and feast in their houses, each on his appointed day, and would send and invite their three sisters to eat and drink with them. So it was, when the days of feasting had run their course, that Job would send and sanctify them, and he would rise early in the morning and offer burnt offerings according to the number of them all. For Job said, "It may be that my sons have sinned and cursed God in their hearts." Thus Job did regularly (Job 1:4–5).

Job does not offer sacrifices for his own sins *per se*, but specifically for the sins of his children. His sacrifices are an example of *his* righteousness. He made sacrifices for his children because they were *his* responsibility. But notice how far he extends his responsibilities. He stands before God on account of what *any* of his children *might* have done in their *hearts*. Unlike many fathers—even Christian fathers—today, Job clearly was not a man to make excuses.

Parents frequently struggle with the issues surrounding personal responsibility because the individualism of our age has taught them to think of responsibility in *either/or* terms instead ·of *both/and* terms. We should not think of the responsibilities of parents and of children as billiard balls which cannot occupy the same place. Instead of thinking that both children and parents are responsible, we think, "Either *he* is responsible or *I* am." Or sometimes we divide the responsibility 50/50 or 70/30. But it must always, we think, add up to 100.

According to the Bible, however, covenants are historical and hierarchical. Responsibility of this kind does not divide, but multiplies and ascends. The covenant responsibility of parents does not diminish the personal responsibility of each child for everything he does and thinks; rather, covenant responsibility strengthens it. Beware of the false dichotomy between individualism and patriarchalism. Guilt is personal and individual. But responsibility is corporate and hierarchical. This is why a child can be guilty of rebelling against God, but his father is not guilty of that sin. At the same time, however, the father is covenantally responsible before God for the rebellion of his child.

Far from being personally condemning, embracing this principle is truly liberating. As Job considered the situation of his home, he assumed responsibility and thus knew exactly what he was supposed to do. This responsibility is *hard*, but not *difficult*. A father must swallow his pride, which is hard to get down, then stand up and do a very simple thing—accept responsibility for the state of his home, including the training and education of his children.

Thinking covenantally achieves great unity. Without it, adversarial thinking develops in the family. "You are over there, and I am over here, and we each have our perspective." Covenantal thinking, by contrast, is the biblical basis for being able to say "we."

We also must remember the sacrifices necessary. Job offered animal sacrifices because he lived prior to Christ. On this side of the cross, we plead only the sacrifice of Christ in our prayer, but as we assume our covenantal responsibility before God, the content of our prayers should be very similar to Job's. We should regularly pray for our children and plead the merits of Christ alone on their behalf. May God be merciful to us! ✒

Trust and Obey

As we work to recover covenantal headship in the home, we need to note that every doctrine lives as it is applied, and no other way. Covenantal headship requires an obedient mind, even when it comes to how our children are educated. *This is not a technique*, it is a *mind of wisdom*. Wisdom is not canned; responsibility cannot be freeze-dried. Parents must always distinguish application from mindless conformity.

Once we learn this principle, it sheds light on the process of all familial decision-making. After a decision is made, the entire family can say that "we are doing thus and such." This is possible only because "we decided to do it." The fact that the decision was made by the covenant head does not affect that unity. If my head decides to go somewhere, my feet go too.

We must lift our covenantal thinking before the Lord, so the best place to put these truths into practice is in our prayer life. Notice that Job did not use his covenantal understanding as a foundation for nagging. He did not show up at the kids' places, saying, "Now you all know how responsible I feel . . ." It was *before the Lord* that he stood and sacrificed. We should do the same for our children.

And we should assume responsibility for them when we rise to our feet, sit in our homes, and walk by the way, surrounding our children with a biblical worldview throughout the day (Deut. 6:4–9), not just on Sunday mornings and Wednesday nights. Being a covenant head means that we are responsible to train and teach them—at all times and in every place—that there is no neutrality regarding God. We either are for Him or against Him in all we do, as we shall see in the next chapter.

4
NOTHING BUT
THE TRUTH

*"The school system that ignores God teaches its pupils to ignore God;
and this is not neutrality. It is the worst form of antagonism, for it judges
God to be unimportant and irrelevant in human affairs. This is atheism."*
—GORDON H. CLARK

Education is one of the most religious things we do.
Consequently, any pretense of religious neutrality in the
process of educating children in some plain-vanilla fashion is a
myth that will lead to enormous confusion. The myth distorts
the nature of knowledge, which is the last thing an educator
should do.

As we reject the myth of neutrality, we must remember that
we are not rejecting neutrality as a bad thing, but rather as an
impossible thing. The problem with the government schools is
that they cannot be neutral, even if the people running them
try their level best. Government schools cannot be neutral any
more than they can fly to the moon or walk on water. But
although they cannot be neutral, they can be confused about
neutrality in education—and so can we.

When we consider the good life under Christ, we must
always remember three great questions. *What is true? What is
good? What is beautiful?* These questions involve the realms of
epistemology (knowledge), ethics, and aesthetics, respectively.
The myth of neutrality is a myth in *each* of these realms.

Ultimately, there is only one realm, the kingdom of our
Lord Jesus Christ. These areas are simply three aspects of Christ's

kingdom. He is Lord of them all. And if He is Lord of them all, there can be no neutrality in any of them.

For or Against Him

The Lord Himself teaches that neutrality is impossible: "He that is not with me is against me; and he that gathereth not with me scattereth abroad" (Matt. 12:30, KJV). We either are going His direction, or we are not. We either are saying what He says, or we contradict it.

Because He is the very Word of God, He is silent about nothing. This means that *everything* we say will be either an *amen* or a disagreement. There is never an instance where we are speaking and He is not. We know this from the very nature of the case. Whenever someone makes all-encompassing claims, then anyone who rejects those claims opposes him.

If Jesus had simply claimed to be the Lord of Palestine, then we could live *here* without regard to Him and not be in opposition to Him. Similarly, we are not in rebellion against the leader of Zimbabwe because we do not even know his name. If our God were simply the god of the hills, no sin would be involved if we worshiped the god of the plains.

But our Lord is Lord of all and says that in every endeavor of life, we either are for Him or against Him. Every word we speak, every thought we think, and every act we commit that is not for Him is against Him.

Lord of Truth

Christ claims to be and is the King of kings and Lord of lords. He told His disciples in the Great Commission that all authority in heaven and earth has been given to Him and that they were therefore to disciple the nations. Thus, *by definition*, anyone or anything (including any institution) that does not acknowledge His authority rebels against it.

Jesus Christ does not just claim authority in some political or civic sense. He is the Lord of everything. He is the Lord of epistemology. He is the Lord of truth. He is the Lord of beauty. He is the Lord of goodness. He is true, beautiful, and good, and He is the only foundation of truth, beauty, and goodness. This means that government schools that do not acknowledge Him are not only in rebellion against His person, they also are in rebellion against those things that are in His right hand.

Why are the government schools full of lies? We cannot answer this question apart from broader questions. Ultimately, government schools are full of lies because they pretend to have truth apart from the Lord of truth.

The Bible repeatedly speaks about Christ as the Lord of truth.

> The Word was made flesh, and dwelt among us, (and we beheld his glory, the glory as of the only begotten of the Father,) *full of grace and truth.* John bare witness of him, and cried, saying, This was he of whom I spake, He that cometh after me is preferred before me: for he was before me. And of his fullness have all we received, and grace for grace. For the law was given by Moses, *but grace and truth came by Jesus Christ* (John 1:14–17, KJV).

John tells us that Christ is full of grace and truth, and that grace and truth come to us only through Him.

On one occasion, Jesus said "to those Jews which believed on him, If ye continue in my word, *then* are ye my disciples indeed; and ye shall know the truth, *and the truth shall make you free*" (John 8:31–32, KJV). The truth He spoke of was not a narrow and truncated "truth," but rather a truth that was all-encompassing. This is the way it had to be. "Jesus saith unto him, *I am* the way, *the truth,* and the life: no man cometh unto the Father, but by me" (John 14:6, KJV). Jesus Christ is the embodiment of truth, and came into the world in order to bear witness to the truth. "Every one that is of the truth heareth my voice" (John 18:37, KJV).

Education and Truth

We cannot approach the truth piecemeal. The demands of truth are all-encompassing, and this means that the duty of education is at the center of their calling as parents. As parents, we must give ourselves away to pass these precious truths on to our children. God's view on this kind of education is worth considering at some length. Deuteronomy says:

Therefore shall ye lay up these my words in your heart and in your soul, and bind them for a sign upon your hand, that they may be as frontlets between your eyes. And *ye shall teach them your children*, speaking of them when thou sittest in thine house, and when thou walkest by the way, when thou liest down, and when thou risest up. And thou shalt write them upon the door posts of thine house, and upon thy gates: That your days may be multiplied, and the days of your children, in the land which the LORD sware unto your fathers to give them, as the days of heaven upon the earth. For if ye shall diligently keep all these commandments which I command you, to do them, *to love the LORD your God*, to walk in all his ways, and to cleave unto him; then will the LORD drive out all these nations from before you, and ye shall possess greater nations and mightier than yourselves (Deut. 11:18–23, KJV).

For parents, love for God and a Christian education for their children are inseparable. We cannot get away from the point by relegating such passages to the realm of religious truth, whatever that is. Statements either conform to reality or they don't. Any school that wants to educate children apart from Christ, the Lord of reality, wants to educate in the realm of unreality, and ultimately prefers lies over the truth. Any school that is not for Christ is against Him. He is the Lord of truth, and no true education exists apart from Him.

If He is not the Lord of all, He is not Lord at all. Call it whatever you like, but education apart from Christ is not Christian education. Apart from the Lord of truth, there is no truth. None at all. But just as He is the Lord of truth, so He also is the Lord of goodness.

5
FOR GOODNESS' SAKE

✝ *"We make men without chests and expect of them virtue and enterprise. We laugh at honour and are shocked to find traitors in our midst."* ✝
—C. S. LEWIS

As we have seen, the good life under Christ reduces to three great questions: What is *true?* What is *good?* What is *beautiful?* And we have noted that neutrality is a myth in each of these realms. Because we have believed the lie that neutrality is possible, we have only confused ourselves in each of these realms. In government schools, we have passed that confusion on, with interest, to the next generation. This is especially evident in the realm of morality.

The Standard

From Scripture we understand that the question of ethics has two sides. That which is good is defined by the character of God Himself, as revealed in His holy law. That which is sinful is defined as whatever transgresses or fails to conform to His law. That which is good is like God. That which is evil is unlike God.

Because of this antithesis between good and evil, our ethical standard will be based either upon the character of God or upon the character of man. If it is based upon the character of God (which for Christians it is), then that ethical standard will reflect certain essential attributes of His character. Because God is unchanging, any standard based upon His character also will be

43

unchanging. Because God is holy, any standard based upon His character will be holy.

If government schools reject the revealed character of God in the Bible as the basis for the ethical instruction they provide to children, then the only option open to them is to teach on the basis of the character of their new god, *demos* (the people). Their law must reflect the character of their god. But *demos* is fickle, utterly changeable. This means that any ethic based upon the will of man must be equally changeable. No fixed standard is possible because men constantly change their minds. And who knows what might happen in the next election?

But because fallen man still bears the image of God and must live in the world God made, he requires a fixed standard. Despite their inability to *account* for a fixed standard, the people still want certain things to remain off limits, such as harming the environment, using politically incorrect speech, and so on. Therefore, the people end up smuggling in absolutes from somewhere while denying they have done so. But because those who are fallen are unholy and sinful, an ethic based on their character will be no different.

Relatively Speaking

Because God is God, men cannot create a truly relativistic world. They can only pretend that this world, with all its built-in absolutes, is somehow relativistic. Absolutes, however, are borrowed from the Christian worldview, then denied in the name of relativism.

As theologian Cornelius Van Til has poignantly shown, the unbeliever vacillates between rationalism and irrationalism. In the same way, the unbeliever careens between a fixed ethic and a *flexible* ethic—whichever suits him. Because our government schools are institutions dedicated to the propagation of unbelief, we find this pattern there, swinging away like a pendulum.

This is why we find a *jihad* against racism, pollution, or global warming in the government schools at one moment, then seconds later, we find the same absolutist zealots insisting that there is no such thing as absolute good or evil when it comes to homosexuality or other "alternative lifestyles." And further, the kids are told that if they do not believe in the relativism dished out to them, they will find themselves doing bad things. Follow this argument closely: It is bad to reject relativism because such rejection suggests that there might be such a thing as "bad." That would be bad.

Rationalism and irrationalism. Absolutism and relativism. All in the same breath. Amazing!

A Way Out

Another option may suggest itself to some who are trying to get off the horns of this irrational dilemma. Why can't government schools simply decline to educate in terms of any ethical standard at all?

The answer should be obvious. No institution can exist without insisting upon some minimal standards of behavior. Tardiness, skipping school, and cheating are always wrong. As the recent history of government schools in this country demonstrates, the standards of government schools may be minimal, but moral anarchy is not an option even for them. Yet all regulations are nothing more than imposed morality. The only questions are *which* morality will be imposed—and *why.*

A Walking Contradiction

Standards are inescapable; they will be imposed. On the one hand, they will either be God-honoring, good, and consistent, or on the other hand, man-serving, sinful, and contradictory.

A few years ago, my son was taking a class from an unbelieving English instructor at the university. One of her driving themes was this kind of self-contradicting relativism. She had the class watch a movie in which the central point was that *everything* is relative: You must not allow anyone to tell you what to do, and you must do what you feel. She let the class know that she thought this liberating relativism was wonderful and was the only way for enlightened students to go.

The class was then assigned a three-page paper on the movie. My son wrote about how he used to be caught up in absolutes, caught in the death grip of fundamentalism, but that the movie had brought him real relief. He had learned from the movie that he should only do what he felt like doing and not allow anyone to tell him what to do. Since he didn't feel like writing a three-page paper just then, he wrote a simple paragraph instead. He was courteous enough about the whole episode. He expressed his gratitude for the lesson, stapled his paragraph written on one page to two blank sheets, and turned in the assignment when due.

When his instructor inevitably confronted him, she said that she was going to give him a failing grade for the paper and that if he didn't rewrite it, she was going to flunk him for the class. When he asked if she saw his point, she said, "You can't take these ideas out to their logical conclusion!" This meant that he was being taught to defy every authority except for *hers*. Relativism must alternate between flexibility on the one hand and arbitrary absolutes, rigidly imposed, on the other.

So ethical relativism means that we are given permission to defy every commandment except for the ones currently in force by those in authority. This kind of relativism makes sure we are free as long as we do what we are told. And this is the "moral universe" that currently rules government schools.

Reaping What We Sow

Schools exist to prepare a future citizenry. In a relativistic society, schools teach relativism. But because society has an interest in self-preservation (however inconsistent), everyone will be appalled at the products put out by the relativistic school system.

We sow the seeds of relativism, then claim to be appalled by its fruit. Amoral sex education classes abound, yet everyone is distressed with what a kid might do in his own self-tutorial or privately arranged *practicum*. A young man takes copious notes in those classes in which he is taught that there is no such thing as a fixed standard of sexual morality. When he is later caught raping or killing someone, he wonders why everyone is so uptight. As C. S. Lewis prophetically put it in *The Abolition of Man*, we laugh at honor and then are shocked to find traitors in our midst.

A Better Way

We tell the kids that life is not worth living, then are surprised at the suicide rate for teens. Teaching ethical relativism is education for fools, by fools (Ps. 14:1). The Bible tells us in no uncertain terms that we are to educate our children so that they love and follow the law of God, fearing His name. Here is what God Himself has to say on this subject:

> Only take heed to thyself, and keep thy soul diligently, lest thou forget the things which thine eyes have seen, and lest they depart from thy heart all the days of thy life: but teach them thy sons, and thy son's sons; specially the day that thou stoodest before the LORD thy God in Horeb, when the LORD said unto me, Gather me the people together, and I will make them hear my words, *that they may learn to fear me* all the days that they shall live upon the earth, *and that they may teach their children* (Deut. 4:9–10, KJV).

When we teach our children how to live, we must do so in the light of God's law, not in the light of recent opinion polls or the latest "balloon juice" served up by the education establishment. Why should our children respect life? Because God spoke to Moses on Sinai and gave His holy law. Why should our children do unto others as they would have done unto them? Because the Lord Jesus Christ said so. Every other foundation for moral behavior is shifting sand. And we all know what happens to houses built on sand.

 Government schools have no firm foundation for teaching the truth or distinguishing right from wrong. They also have no firm foundation for setting true beauty before our children. Like truth and goodness, beauty cannot be taught apart from God.

6
A REAL
BEAUTY

"The end then of learning is to repair the ruins of our first parents by regaining to know God aright, and out of that knowledge to love Him, to imitate Him, to be like Him, as we may the nearest by possessing our souls of true virtue, which being united to the heavenly grace of faith, makes up the highest perfection."
—JOHN MILTON

Only Christian education can provide a standard for fixed and absolute truth, and only a biblical course of instruction can set a standard for distinguishing right from wrong. But what about beauty?

The first problem we encounter is defining our terms. When we talk about beauty, we are talking about aesthetics, and we cannot talk about aesthetics in general (even in the context of education) without talking about art. The phrase "modern art" is common enough now but will eventually be dated and inaccurate. So will "postmodern." To remove the phrase from the constraints of time, I suggest calling it "autonomous art." When we as Christians consider the government schools, we must reject the notion that beauty is relative, insisting rather that it is an objective measurement for autonomous art. As such, beauty is capable of revealing that government schools are ugly and that they have an ugly story to tell our children.

Painting the Backdrop

But first, we must paint the backdrop. "Objectivists" in the realm of aesthetics must guard themselves. Popular reactions may or may not indicate a real problem for an autonomous approach to art and beauty.

True, the critic's job may be made easier by such reactions if he is playing to a friendly audience. If the critic happens to be right, this is well and good. But popular reaction has in the past targeted artistic endeavors that are now universally applauded. The masses do not like what is ugly, but as creatures of habit, they also may not like what is unusual. So what is the aesthetic interest *for*? Does art have a functional role within culture? We must consider the problems with democratic aesthetics, popular taste, and the test of time. All these questions must be *at the center* of any discussion of true education.

Tragically, aesthetic relativism completely dominates the government school system, and it has even made significant inroads in many Christian schools. This aesthetic relativism poses the greatest possible threat to Christian families, far greater than is posed by the assaults on truth and goodness. Most Christians have enough discernment to recognize assaults on truth and goodness. But assaults on beauty are pervasive and go largely unrecognized. Because government schools have successfully established their unbelieving and autonomous aesthetic theory, we have young people taught "well"—they dress in ugly clothes, listen to ugly music, and generally surround themselves with barrenness. And they do so because of how they were educated.

Autonomous man wants to make up his own standards of truth, his own standards of goodness, and, not surprisingly, his own standards of beauty. Just as this autonomy has destroyed all coherent notions of truth and goodness, it has destroyed the standard of beauty. Children who attend government schools are taught that no objective beauty exists. The building surrounding them often is functional-ugly. Their peers are slovenly dressed. And they graduate with souls that look like beef jerky.

So what are the central theological problems with autonomous aesthetics? If there is *no neutrality*, then there is no such thing as truly autonomous art. It cannot sustain or defend itself. If idolatry is a sin, then art for art's sake—autonomous art—cannot be defended. And if beauty is not determined by fads, then the autonomous artistic community has lost its authority. In short, if we remove all the sin and have nothing *sustainable* left, then we have learned something about autonomous art.

An Ugly Story

This brings us to the aesthetic problem inherent in the government school system. Government schools educate kids in the tenets of agnostic materialism—an ugly story that will deform those who believe it.

As institutions devoted to an ugly story, government schools are built like ugly knowledge factories. Students are not uplifted by the architecture of the schools they attend. Just compare schools built five years ago with schools built a century ago. Architectural shapes and forms are an essential part of any cultural education.

Surrounded by such impersonal ugliness, students reassert their humanity by consistently running in the direction of the bizarre. Modernist architecture leads to postmodern student attire. Thus, the authorities and the rebels are both doing the same thing, even when they do not see it that way.

Another expression of aesthetic relativism on the part of government school students is found in the music they listen to and surround themselves with. (Again, this rebellion is not *against* their government education, but rather, is the application of it.) Some might wonder why I am addressing music in a book on education, but think about it for moment. Few things have as deep an impact on young people as their music, and the music they listen to flows directly from how they are taught to think about things like music. And where do they learn how to think about such things?

As God's people, the task before us is always to think like Christians in everything we do. In more than just a few instances, this task means that we have to swim against the tide. But having a Christian worldview does not mean sitting in the La-Z-Boy, thinking great thoughts. Everything must come down to application. One of the things that shapes the thinking in young people today is their music. What sort of music do the government schools tolerate? More important, what principles of aesthetic discrimination (or lack of it) do they teach young people throughout the course of their studies? The question is always *by what standard*? God gives us the aesthetic standard:

> ⚹ Finally, brethren, whatever things are true, whatever things are noble, whatever things are just, whatever things are pure, whatever things are lovely, whatever things are of good report, if there is any virtue and if there is anything praiseworthy; meditate on these things (Phil. 4:8). ⚹

For Christians, the goal is to concentrate on what is lovely. Admittedly, students are not usually allowed to listen to Nine Inch Nails during math class at government schools. But students listen to such stuff on their *own* time as a result of how they have been trained to think. The Bible teaches that music, like every other aesthetic endeavor, must aspire to the lovely.

Having Good Sense

Aesthetics is not a simple subject, but it is an important one. A Christian education is necessary precisely because the ability to make aesthetic distinctions takes work, often hard work. But solid food belongs to those who are of full age, that is, those who by reason of use have their senses exercised to discern both good and evil (Heb. 5:14). Christian parents who desire to offer their children a distinctively Christian education must be wise and discerning in how they go about their task. To avoid this whole subject becoming bad business from start to finish, Christian parents must have a few things, the first of which is character.

Character. -From the outset, Christian parents must have character. God has given them authority in the home, and if a government school is teaching in a way that undermines their authority, parents must wield their authority to take their kids out of that school. God did not give authority to parents so that they would nervously avoid using it. When parents make decisions for the household, they should do so without apology. If it requires apology, it should not be done in the first place. A submissive spirit toward God means that parents must make authoritative decisions. This means they must have the character to wield submissive authority with love for their children. ◄

Courage.-Christian parents must also have aesthetic courage. In many profound ways, Christians are at war with modernity. Of course, this does not mean that we reject every feature of modern life, but it does mean taking a stand against all modern idolatries.►Taking this kind of stand can be costly, and parents need the grace of God to strengthen them. Their standard for action must not be: "What will people think?" Instead, we know that "God hath not given us the spirit of fear; but of power, and of love, and of a sound mind" (2 Tim. 1:7, KJV).

Confidence.►Parents must also have confidence. When they come to difficult decisions, they must shake loose of the world's propaganda that says parents are terminally "unhip" and are unfit to pass judgment on aesthetics.► Parents know far more about the world than their kids do. The concept of "cool" is nothing but sleight-of-hand propaganda designed to make parents forget what they know.

Comprehensive Thinking. Parents must also embrace the duty of thinking comprehensively.►The responsibility of parents involves *everything* that is going into their children's minds. This means that evaluating what the kids are listening to must not be superficial, e.g., merely seeing whether a CD has any "bad words" on it. Parents must not be afraid to apply aesthetic judgments, judgments about their child's maturity, and so forth. ◄

What It All Comes Down To

So we have considered just one small aspect of a child's education—the music he listens to. As mentioned earlier, everything comes down to application. This question of music is simply one of many areas calling for Christian parents to *think*. We must deal in like fashion with other situations that arise. But at the heart of all such issues is the question of who has been teaching our children how to think about the world.

As parents make appropriate decisions, they must avoid distractions. The Christian world has no shortage of bogus information on the topic of rock and roll. For some, the backbeat is a matter of major concern. Others exhibit a panicky fear about the messages back-masked into the music. Leave it to Christians to be more concerned about gibberish backwards than wickedness frontward. The issue is sin, not rock music. The issue is wickedness, not a backbeat. The issue is aesthetic standards, not superficial traditional standards.

~ When removing a child from government schools and from ungodly influence, the parent must avoid all forms of legalism. — If parents take a stand on something for reasons of piety—and the only reason they can give for it is "just because"—then they are teaching legalism—rule-making detached from the Word of God. At this point, intentions do not matter. We have no authority to go beyond the Word of God. On the other hand, young people need to be reminded that legalism is not to be defined as any decision their parents make.

~ Parents must also avoid ignorance and not make blind decisions. If they take the trouble to sit down and go over song lyrics with their children, they often lose the debate because of their insufficient knowledge. Parents express doubts and ask questions instead of checking it out for themselves. ~

But suppose parents just yank their kid from government school, enroll him in a Christian school, only to find that their teenager comes home with a borrowed CD by some Christian group that is simply a sanitized imitation. The evangelical subculture has no shortage of cheap imitations of whatever the world is currently doing (or more often, what the world did five years ago!). We do not solve our problem by trying to come up with baptized ungodliness.

Talking Together

This brings us to the essential point. Parents should be situated *so that they can teach their kids.* If music is part of your family's life (and it should be), then it should be part of your conversation. Talk about the world in the light of Scripture, and do so regularly. If children are in government schools, these discussions are far more likely to be arguments as the parents (unsuccessfully) try to undo the damage that has been done in their child's mind. In too many situations, the damage is not even apparent to the parents until it is too late to do much about it.

In good family discussions, in concert with a good Christian school, parents hold their kids accountable to learn. The kids must not be allowed to argue, "It is not that bad because . . ." If our children cannot say what is wrong with an objectionable album, they are unprotected and *uneducated*. Parents should be looking for clarity of thought from their children, not excuses or rationalizations.

So there are really only two alternatives, and both of them can be embraced only as part of a comprehensive Christian education. Use the music to teach, or use it for landfill (Acts 19:18–20). Don't be afraid to throw out lousy music.

We are called to surround our children with the Lord their God as the standard of truth, goodness, and beauty. Of course, this is an important part of raising our children in the nurture and admonition of the Lord—the subject of the next chapter.

7
NURTURE AND ADMONITION

X *"To commit our children to the care of irreligious persons is
to commit lambs to the superintendency of wolves."* X
—TIMOTHY DWIGHT

We live in a superficial era. Therefore, when we say that we are
biblically required to give our children a Christian education,
some believers demand that we produce a verse saying in so
many words that "government schools are sinful." Because a
Bible passage is not written in exactly those words, these believers think the Bible has not made this point.

Getting the Point

When we make these exacting demands of the Bible, we are like
those who think that computer fraud is not prohibited because
computers are not mentioned in the Bible, or that murder with
a .357 magnum is okay for the same reason. The biblical requirement to give kids a Christian education is not stated using our
modern vocabulary, but it is stated *expressly* and unequivocally.

- In Ephesians, fathers are commanded to provide their children with a biblical *education*. "And, ye fathers, provoke not
your children to wrath: but bring them up in the nurture and
admonition of the Lord" (Eph. 6:4, KJV). The word translated
admonition here is *paideia*. It not only includes what we call
education, but it also requires a biblical culture surrounding
and supporting that process. While the command cannot be
fully met outside of a Christian civilization, the text certainly

forbids fathers from providing their children with a *non*-Christian education.

The statement is clear and is not far from "thou shalt provide thy children with a Christian education." The verse flatly excludes sending Christian children to an unbelieving institution and allowing them to be surrounded with unbelieving peers. The children sent to government schools read unbelieving textbooks explained mostly by unbelieving teachers. Believing teachers are still hired at government schools, but only with the stipulation that they don't allow their faith to *show*. Christian teachers can still be employed, but only with the rigidly enforced proviso that their light stay under a bushel.

Bringing children up in the education of the Lord involves far more than being worried about their friends, or having a chat every six months or so about how things are going at school. Even if a child wanted, he couldn't adequately answer such questions precisely because he has not received a biblical education in the first place. In other words, the child has not been equipped to give an accurate report on the education he is receiving because he has not received the biblical education that would enable him to give such a report. If he doesn't know what an anti-supernatural bias is, he won't know when it hits him alongside the head, much less know how to tell Mom or Dad that he has a splitting headache from the whole episode.

Teaching Them Diligently

The same standard applies in the Old Testament. God issues the greatest commandment—to love Him with heart, soul, mind, and strength—specifically in the context of educating children.

Parents are responsible before God to ensure that children grow up in an environment *dominated* by the Word of God. This responsibility means, among other things, that our children are to grow up thinking about everything from a biblical standpoint and in contrast to unbiblical standpoints. We are to teach them to think *antithetically—this* is *true*, and *that* is *false*.

> Hear, O Israel: The LORD our God is one LORD: And thou shalt love the LORD thy God with all thine heart, and with all thy soul, and with all thy might. And

> these words, which I command thee this day, shall be in thine heart: And thou shalt teach them diligently unto thy children, and shalt talk of them when thou sittest in thine house, and when thou walkest by the way, and when thou liest down, and when thou risest up. And thou shalt bind them for a sign upon thine hand, and they shall be as frontlets between thine eyes. And thou shalt write them upon the posts of thy house, and on thy gates (Deut. 6:4–9, KJV).

Christian parents ignore this command when they send their children to government schools. What do those children hear when they sit down at desks purchased by the taxpayer? That men are evolved from primordial goo, that *Heather Has Two Mommies*, and that all we need to do is to make sure we recycle. What do they hear when they *rise up*? Assorted blasphemies and foul language on the playground. What do they read when they *walk along the way*? A big sign at the entrance of the school proclaiming that it is a drug-free zone.

In short, the very thing God requires in Deuteronomy 6 is patently ignored by parents who send their children to government schools. For much of their waking hours, the only words these children hear are the words of men who live in opposition to the Word of God.

Image is Everything

When wicked men sought to entrap Jesus in a debate over taxes, He instructed his hearers to pay tax money with Caesar's image on it to Caesar:

> Jesus perceived their wickedness, and said, Why tempt ye me, ye hypocrites? Show me the tribute money. And they brought unto him a penny. And he saith unto them, Whose is this image and superscription? They say unto him, Caesar's. Then saith he unto them, Render therefore unto Caesar the things which are Caesar's; and unto God the things that are God's. When they had heard these words, they marvelled, and left him, and went their way (Matt. 22:18–22, KJV).

We often overlook one important implication of Christ's teaching: We not only should render to Caesar what is Caesar's, but we also must not render to Caesar what is God's.

What should we use to determine "what is God's" in this context? Who bears God's image—the *imago Dei?* The answer certainly includes our children. This means that our children may not be rendered to Caesar. But the history of the world teaches us that this is one of the first things Caesar demands.

In our nation, we rendered our children to Caesar long before the levels of taxation became oppressive. Nonetheless, we followed the same pattern predicted by Samuel for Israel when Israel demanded a king (1 Sam. 8). The children were taken first as slaves to the king. In a similar way, by sending our kids to government schools, we are giving them to "Caesar" as slaves to our cultural godlessness. But if we acquiesce in that tragedy, why draw the line anywhere else?

When we take the Deuteronomy 6 and 1 Samuel 8 passages together, the conclusion is inescapable: *Christian parents who send Christian children to government schools when those children are uneducated and unprepared are rendering to Caesar what is God's.*

Christian kids should receive a distinctively Christian education because the Bible expressly requires it in a variety of passages. We have seen two of these passages in this chapter. In the next chapter, we will see another—the command to love the Lord with all our mind. This is not just a command given to us as parents. As we train up our children, we are to teach them *everything* our Lord and their Lord has commanded us (Matt. 28:20), for He is not only our God, but also the God of our children after us (Acts 2:39). So we are commanded to ensure that our children grow up to love the Lord their God with all their mind.

8
WITH ALL YOUR MIND

✂ *"Let every student be plainly instructed and earnestly pressed to consider well the main end of his life and studies is to know God and Jesus Christ which is eternal life, John 17:3, and therefore to lay Christ in the bottom, as the only foundation of all sound knowledge and learning."*
—HARVARD, RULES AND PRECEPTS ✂

Christian education is mandatory if we walk in obedience to the greatest commandment. "Jesus said unto him, Thou shalt love the Lord thy God with all thy heart, and with all thy soul, *and with all thy mind*" (Matt. 22:37, KJV). We cannot dismiss the imperative given to us in this text.

Loving God in Everything

We need to meditate on this text for more than just a moment. Our children come into this world not knowing how to do anything with their minds, and God places on them the mandate of loving Him with all their minds. How and when are they going to learn this lesson?

The world is a sinful and fallen place, so this task is daunting. How can our children learn how to love God if they are taught by men and women who do *not* love God? Will our children learn to love God with their minds if the people responsible for training their minds have no idea what this passage means? And even if some teachers at government schools happen to be Christians, how will our children learn how to love God with all their minds when those teachers who do love God are prohibited by law from teaching them anything about Him when school is in session?

Loving God with all our minds does not mean that we are to love God with our minds merely from the time on Sunday morning when we enter the church until we return home from church. We are called to love God at all times and all places—whenever we use our minds. *All* our minds, *all* the time. We must love God as we read novels, love Him as we watch movies, love Him as we plant our gardens, and love Him when we solve engineering problems. We must love God in how we think about *everything*. This commandment is set before us, and one of the first ways we apply it is in the way we instruct our children.

Something's Missing

Education is the process of learning to think about everything. To leave out our obligation to love God in the process of education is, to use an old example, like putting on a production of *Hamlet* while omitting the role of the prince of Denmark.

When our children attend government schools, they are told to learn math, but not to learn the central thing about math—that God is a God of order and that in Him all things consist. They are told to learn history, but not the most important thing about history—that Jesus Christ lived a perfect life, died an efficacious death, rose powerfully, and ascended majestically to the right hand of the Father.

When God is excluded from the classroom, we are not merely remaining silent about God. We are teaching children that they may safely disregard Him. Whether or not God exists, the lesson goes, His existence is irrelevant to what we are doing *here*. So when God is omitted, we are not silent about Him; rather, we are teaching the children in the most convincing way possible that God is irrelevant. *They* can safely omit Him when it is convenient to do so.

The classroom exists to shape and disciple minds. When we consider whether government schools are an option for Christians, we must ask about the shape of the mold into which our children are being placed. With their children as disciples,

62

parents have to ask, "*Who* is the master? And does he serve the same Master as the parents?"

Given the subjectivism of our age, many parents assume that their duty is simply to get their kids to love Jesus with all their hearts, which they think can be done if their kids attend church every Sunday. Perhaps they even have devotions at home.

The assumption that the "heart" can be isolated from the mind is questionable, but let us grant it for the sake of discussion. This state of affairs would fulfill only part of the command. When we realize that the command includes learning how to love God throughout the course of every intellectual pursuit Monday through Friday, the picture changes entirely.

The task of learning to think like a Christian in every area of life is a serious and demanding one, even when both parents and teachers understand this task and are committed to it. But if teachers are not committed to this task or are hostile to it, the task is impossible. If you want your children to learn to play the violin, do you apprentice them to a blacksmith? If you want them to learn to master art, do you apprentice them to a football coach? If you want them to think like believers, do you apprentice them to unbelievers or silenced believers?

The Christian Mind

Christian children cannot learn to love the Lord their God with all their minds until they are trained to have a Christian mind. Such training requires a distinctively Christian education.

Without doubt, Africa needs more missionaries, but that is no reason for parents to put their tots on an airplane to be "salt and light" in Africa, regardless of whether the flight attendants would be willing to help them off the plane in Nairobi. Africa needs missionaries *who have been trained and prepared* for what they will encounter, not small children sent off on what would invariably become a hopeless children's crusade.

A school is where students *receive* training. They go to school because they have not been trained already. In short, the only Christian students prepared to run the gauntlet of unbelieving education are those who have already received a thorough

Christian education. In my contact with hundreds of Christian students through the years, I have encountered a good number who are capable of defending the faith and taking on unbelieving instructors by the time they get to college. Before that time, each of them needed to be trained in defending the Christian worldview, and after that time, most of them still need biblical instruction and continued preparation.

Too often parents measure success by a truly odd criterion. "My child attended public schools, and he graduated with his faith intact. He still attends church." In other words, we think the educational process is vindicated simply because some students *survive* it. But if I were to hit myself in the head repeatedly with a hammer and survive, my survival would not really be an argument in favor of the practice. The true measure is how well the students think God's thoughts with their minds moment by moment.

To understand how to think God's thoughts moment by moment, we need to understand that we are called to take every thought captive to the obedience of Christ, the subject to which we now turn.

9
EVERY THOUGHT CAPTIVE

"A truly Christian education is possible only when Christian education underlies not a part, but all, of the curriculum of the school. True learning and true piety go hand in hand, and Christianity embraces the whole of life—those are great central convictions that underlie the Christian school."
—J. GRESHAM MACHEN

Christians should give their children a distinctively Christian education because they are called to take every thought captive to the obedience of Christ. Let me explain.

Setting Sights Too Low

Consider the example of Paul, who took as his life-mission to cast "down imaginations, and every high thing that exalteth itself against the knowledge of God, and [bring] into captivity every thought to the obedience of Christ" (2 Cor. 10:5, KJV). Everything is subject to Christ as Lord, even our very thoughts. God calls us to cast down *everything* that sets itself against Him and to bring *everything* to the obedience to Christ—down to every thought.

In contrast to this divine calling to take every thought captive, many evangelical activists, including those who want to "reform" the government schools, set their sights far too low. Rather than dealing with errant thinking, many activists frequently want to "earn respect," or gain "a place at the table" with those who are at war with God. Such evangelicals expect to have limited conflict and do not think in terms of a constant, total war. They want to cast down only some imaginations and some things that exalt themselves against God. They want to take some thoughts captive to the obedience of Christ.

We must ask such believers, "Why do you want a place at the table? Who are the guests? Who is the cook? What is he serving today?"—If we think as biblical Christians, we will refuse to sit quietly at any table where the Lord Jesus Christ does not have the place of ultimate honor at the head. ⸺

This goal may sound militant to some and out of step with the "pluralism" surrounding us in almost every discussion of public issues today. But the real question is not whether it sounds militant, because classical theology itself distinguishes between the *militant* church on earth overcoming unrighteousness for the cause of God and truth and the *triumphant* church in heaven coming face to face with the Lord of righteousness and truth. The real question is whether it is *true*. What do we have in common with those who want to educate without referring to God? We all know the answer, but some evangelicals try to downplay it.

Converting Government Schools?

A fundamental question, however, needs to be asked of all Christians who seek to reform government schools. The question concerns the final goal behind all intermediate goals, whether it be allowing prayer in the classroom, removing offensive sex education classes, or resisting evolution in biology. *Do those who attempt to reform government schools intend to make government schools explicitly Christian?*

If the answer is *yes*, then secularists have all the more reason to reject our proposed reforms because we would be imposing our beliefs on them at taxpayer expense. But at least the reformer would have the advantage of rejecting the false gods of agnosticism or principled relativism in the schools. At least this kind of reformer recognizes that the humanism taught in government schools is an established religion. And because Christianity is the true religion, it should be the one that is institutionally established, if *any* are to be established in this way.

It would be difficult to find a Christian who overtly supported the public establishment of false religions. Christians tout such ideas only when they have been duped into believing that the false religion in question is not a religion at all. In short, Christians go along with this sort of reasoning only when they fall for the myth of neutrality.

When a reformer advocates making government schools into Christian schools, the question shifts away from whether education is neutral and becomes quite a different one altogether: *Which form of Christian establishment by the state should we pursue—institutional or non-institutional?*

The Big Lie

In discussing whether we should reform government schools so that they are Christian, the answer is rarely yes. Those who want to reform government schools never have as their goal making those schools into explicitly Christian institutions. Far from taking every thought captive, most Christians have settled for simply tidying up the secularism of the government schools. All they really want is to be "left alone." They don't want their "values assaulted." All they want to believe is the big lie their parents believed about government schools in the fifties.

This big lie is that education can be "religion-neutral." The government will provide all the neutral facts, we were told, and parents can add their own values at home, as though the Christian faith were not a world-and-life view and could be reduced to an intellectual seasoning or a condiment. Because Christians swallow the myth of neutrality, they do not see established government schools as institutions that propagate an established religion. They see them as established propagators of "neutral" facts to which everyone agrees.

We are assured that Buddhists, Muslims, Christians, agnostics, and atheists all agree that two and two make four and that America declared her independence from Great Britain in 1776. Such facts are neutral, the claim goes, and each faith system can then set the context for those facts at home or at church. We fail to see that unless Jesus Christ is seated at the right hand of God the Father, two and two do not make four. He is the One in whom all things consist (Col. 1:17).

As skeptical moderns, we like to assume that there is such a thing as brute factuality—naked facts that no one knows and that everyone approaches for the first time. We also like to assume that these facts would remain true even if Christ were not Lord. But given the nature of God and His sovereignty over all things, there is no such thing as naked truth. For Christians, all facts are what they are because of how God interprets them. If He did not interpret them this way, then we cannot generate any legitimate alternative from some other source.

Simplistically, if God were not the Creator, then Columbus could not have discovered America because both he and the American continent would still be uncreated. If God were not the Creator, then the War for Independence could not have happened. There would be nothing to shoot at. If Christ were not Lord, then two plus two could not equal four. Two *what*? Four *what*?

Our knowledge must always follow after God's. Put another way, we are not capable of thinking any genuinely new thoughts. Every fact has been thought before—by God—and is interpreted by Him. Solid education, therefore, is the process of learning how to think God's thoughts after Him. Any process that denies these (self-evident) truths is inherently confused, and consequently, we must not place our children in the midst of that confusion to be educated.

We also must be wary of handing our children over to a godless or, at best, an agnostic state. The children of Israel clamored for a king and were warned that the king would lay claim to their children. The same thing happens today for those who want to be coddled by the state. Like the children of Israel, we should be careful what we ask for, because we just might get it.

10
BE CAREFUL
WHAT YOU ASK

*✗ "We are being taxed to support schools that are systematically
liquidating our most cherished beliefs." ✗*
—PAUL VITZ

From Caesar to Dewey, from Nebuchadnezzar to Mann, those who have given ultimate authority to the state have consistently coveted other people's children. Because statists see the state as the highest level to which man attains, they naturally bring the best and the brightest to serve the state and see education as the means to that end.

Samuel's Sons

When Samuel warned the Israelites about the dire consequences of desiring a king like the other nations, he warned them in ways that should shock us. First, let's set the scene in which the warning takes place:

> It came to pass, when Samuel was old, that he made his sons judges over Israel. Now the name of his first-born was Joel; and the name of his second, Abiah: they were judges in Beersheba. And his sons walked not in his ways, but turned aside after lucre, and took bribes, and perverted judgment (1 Sam. 8:1–3, KJV).

The problem began with Samuel, who didn't discipline his sons, who were then unfaithful to God. The people were unfaithful too, as the Lord makes clear, but Samuel had given the people an excuse by how he brought up his sons. The Scripture is clear that his sons were guilty as charged. They were money-hungry, took bribes, and perverted judgment.

Setting the Stage

Joel and Abiah set the stage for the statism to follow:

> Then all the elders of Israel gathered themselves together, and came to Samuel unto Ramah, and said unto him, Behold, thou art old, and thy sons walk not in thy ways: now make us a king to judge us like all the nations. But the thing displeased Samuel, when they said, Give us a king to judge us. And Samuel prayed unto the LORD (1 Sam. 8:4–6, KJV).

One sin does not justify another, so Samuel's failure as a father did not justify the Israelites asking for a king. They asked specifically for a king like "all the nations" (v. 5). The problem was not that they wanted a ruler *unlike* Samuel's sons, but rather that they wanted one *like* the pagan nations. In effect, they used mild corruption as an excuse to ask for major corruption. God told Samuel to inform the people that they would get what they wanted, but He wanted Samuel to tell them exactly what that request would entail.

What happens when a free people come to be ruled like all the other nations?

> The LORD said unto Samuel, Hearken unto the voice of the people in all that they say unto thee: for they have not rejected thee, but they have rejected me, that I should not reign over them. According to all the works which they have done since the day that I brought them up out of Egypt even unto this day, wherewith they have forsaken me, and served other gods, so do they also unto thee. Now therefore hearken unto their voice: howbeit yet protest solemnly unto them, and show them the manner of the king that shall reign over them (1 Sam. 8:7–9, KJV).

The excuse for rebellion provided by Samuel's sons was not a good one. God saw right through it. They were not really rejecting Samuel's sons; they were calling for a system that would involve far more corruption than was exhibited by those two men. The people were really rejecting Samuel, by their own words an *honest* judge, and, as such, they also rejected the God of Samuel.

Uncle Sam and Your Children

God told Samuel to grant their request, but to make sure they walked into the tyranny with their eyes open. They would be shown what rule looks like when God is not involved in it.

> Samuel told all the words of the LORD unto the people that asked of him a king. And he said, This will be the manner of the king that shall reign over you: He will take your sons, and appoint them for himself, for his chariots, and to be his horsemen . . . And he will take your daughters to be confectionaries, and to be cooks, and to be bakers (1 Sam. 8:10,11,13, KJV).

The first thing Samuel tells the people is that the king will *take their children.* He will use them for the various needs the state might have. In Samuel's day, the need included charioteers and runners to go before the chariots. Sons would be taken to become men of war. Sons would also be taken to work in the king's fields and in munitions factories. Daughters would be taken as confectioners, cooks, and bakers.

In modern terms, we see how this works. Today, statists see the education of children as a matter of public policy. What does the country need? More mathematicians? The cry goes out for mathematics programs in the schools. More scientists? And on it goes.

This has been a consistent feature of statism throughout history. The first claim is made upon the next generation—*upon the children*. We can see that we live under an ungodly political system by how readily our politicians speak about "our children." After all, we have been told, "it takes a village to raise a child."

Taxing Demands

Statists are not content just to take our children. Other economic consequences necessarily follow:

> He will take your fields, and your vineyards, and your oliveyards, even the best of them, and give them to his servants. And he will take the tenth of your seed, and of your vineyards, and give to his officers, and to his servants. And he will take your menservants, and your maidservants, and your goodliest young men, and your asses, and put them to his work. He will take the tenth of your sheep: and ye shall be his servants (1 Sam. 8:14–17, KJV).

We may categorize these as property claims. The most interesting thing about this prediction is that the state rises up in an attempt to rival God. God claims ten percent of our increase in the tithe. The fact that the state would claim the same amount (an outrageous level in Samuel's thinking) shows that the state wants to put itself on a par with the living God. When taxation meets or exceeds 10 percent, we should identify that as the biblical threshold of economic tyranny.

But instead, these days we would be very happy if we could get back to that "low" level of taxation. That which appalled Samuel as economic despotism we would probably hail as radical and libertarian tax reform. We are so deep in the dungeon that having a jail cell with a window seems like freedom to us. A major part of the economic tax oppression we face is to foot the bill for government schools. The fact that our school system does not educate very well does not mean that it is inexpensive.

Falling on Deaf Ears

Samuel did not stop with the bleak consequences we have already seen. Under divine inspiration, he went on to proclaim:

> Ye shall cry out in that day because of your king which ye shall have chosen you; and the LORD will not hear you in that day (1 Sam. 8:18, KJV).

When that time of judgment rolls around, *nothing* seems to bring relief. Many of us have probably seen more than one brochure for a conference on "Restoring America," and they all seem to quote 2 Chronicles 7:14: "If My people who are called by My name . . ." These conferences provide a current example of people crying out to God, and, judging from the results to this point, God does not appear to be listening. As it says in 1 Samuel 8:18, the Lord "will not hear you in that day." The Lord does not hear because our repentance is superficial; anyone can whine about the *consequences* of sin. Most attempts to reform the government school system do not constitute true repentance, but are nothing more than attempts to get back to an earlier point in our disobedience, back to when we were sowing, not reaping.

Taking the Plunge

The disobedience of the Israelites was certainly willful:

> Nevertheless the people refused to obey the voice of Samuel; and they said, Nay; but we will have a king over us; that we also may be like all the nations; and that our king may judge us, and go out before us, and fight our battles. And Samuel heard all the words of the people, and he rehearsed them in the ears of the LORD. And the LORD said to Samuel, Hearken unto their voice, and make them a king. And Samuel said unto the men of Israel, Go ye every man unto his city (1 Sam. 8:19–22, KJV).

As the psalmist puts it, God granted their request, but sent leanness to their souls (Ps. 106:15). In this passage from 1 Samuel, we see that statism is not a modern development. It did not come about because of the Industrial Revolution or the onset of modernity. Rather, statism results from people seeking to be pagan in their modes and methods of governing themselves. When they take this route, the state always and immediately assumes a parental responsibility for children. The state may want to call up the children for varied purposes, and therefore, wants to make sure that they are "ready" when called. Consequently, the state has a vested interest in educating our children to suit its purposes.

We have only two options: We may be governed by the Word of God or by the words of men. If we reject the Word of God, we will always find that the words of men come down to dismal and very similar results. This is the nature of unbelief. Statist demands on adults always result in statist demands for the control of the education of future adults. When a pagan society is primitive, the demands are not made from a distance. In a pagan village, the demand of the collective may be every bit as sweeping as it is in a modern state, but it is not made from hundreds of miles away. But when any empire is born, the demands remain great and are applied from a distance.

For example, in Plato's *Republic*, the philosopher sees great value in the authorities maintaining complete and utter control over the process of education. One of the more obvious features of pagan thinking is that the ownership of the state over children is simply assumed. This is what it is like in all the "other nations." They may be great or small, modern or ancient. It does not matter. They will take your sons and daughters.

But modern Christians are accustomed to thinking of history in *evolutionary* terms instead of *antithetical* terms. We believe that our current method of government education is at the tail end of a long chain of historical inevitabilities, rather than thinking of it as one of only two possible options. Compromised by the dogma of evolution, we think that educational faithfulness, while good, is still a dinosaur. This faithfulness may occasionally be applauded, but not for its realism. By contrast, we must see that government schools were in no way made necessary by the advent of science. Just because education is faithful to Scripture does not make it unrealistic.

Choose This Day

Faced with this reality, we have only two choices: We may govern ourselves with the Lord as our King, or we may govern ourselves like the other nations.

Of course, we are not saying that there are no variations on the theme of statist education. The little red schoolhouse may be painted blue. But the worldview alternative is always the same: Will our children be educated the way God instructs us to educate them, or will we imitate "other nations" as we educate them?

Because we moderns think in evolutionary terms, we think of educational *progress* instead of simple education. In the evolutionary world, everything is in flux, and anything might evolve into anything else. In the antithetical and biblical world, education is the process of passing on a believing culture, *which is antithetical* to all unbelieving cultures. The biblical educator says *this*, not *that*. The evolutionary educator says *now*, not *then*. The biblical educator says *right*, not *wrong*, while the evolutionary educator says *current*, not *outdated*.

What do you say? And what are the consequences of making the wrong choice? We take up this sober topic next.

11
WHERE JUDGMENT MUST BEGIN

⚔ *"Cursed be all learning that is contrary to the cross of Christ."* ⚔
—*REV. JONATHAN DICKINSON,*
PRINCETON UNIVERSITY'S FIRST PRESIDENT

Because Christian parents have drifted into an evolutionary approach to life and education, we have now awakened to find the hand of God upon us and our children. Our culture is currently under judgment, and not surprisingly, these judgments are also found in government schools. When the hand of God falls on a culture, it does not affect only those who are eighteen and older. When God judges, He judges a people.

Further, these things are not just "happening" to us. The world is not a machine, grinding mindlessly away. The world is governed according to the wisdom of God, and He tells us in the Bible how these things generally go.

> Now it shall come to pass, if you diligently obey the voice of the LORD your God, to observe carefully all His commandments which I command you today, that the LORD your God will set you high above all nations of the earth (Deut. 28:1).

How does God judge a culture? Too often we assume that divine judgments are only other-worldly. But this is not at all how Scripture speaks of divine judgments. You may have seen some of these judgments from time to time in your newspaper. You may have seen some of them posted on the bulletin board at your child's school. But long before these problems appeared in our midst, they were written in the Book. We will explore just a few of them.

Adversarial Rulers

We first see the problem of adversarial rulers.

> Therefore the wrath of the LORD was kindled against His people, so that He abhorred His own inheritance. And He gave them into the hand of the Gentiles, and those who hated them ruled over them (Ps. 106:40–41).

Rulers who hate the people they rule are a rod in the hand of God. We see this problem throughout the entire government school system. Do tax-funded educators warmly receive the concerns expressed by Christian parents? Go to the next school board meeting and object to some gross and obscene library book, and you will find yourself pilloried as a fundamentalist beetlewit the next day on the front page of the newspaper, wallowing in your opposition to truth, justice, the First Amendment, and probably Huck Finn.

Those who control the machinery of government education in this country have contempt for Christian parents. But this is not primarily their doing. Note that in Psalm 106, the Lord abhorred His own inheritance. *He gave them over*. The reason the National Education Association doesn't listen is because God has turned Christian parents over to their adversaries.

Bygone Blessings

Another great sign of God's judgment is a loss of blessing regarding our children:

> As for Ephraim, their glory shall fly away like a bird; no birth, no pregnancy, and no conception! Though they bring up their children, yet I will bereave them to the last man . . . so Ephraim will bring out his children to the murderer. Give them, O LORD; what will You give? Give them a miscarrying womb and dry breasts! (Hos. 9:11–14).

God has taken a love for fruitfulness away from us so we lose our children to barrenness (both artificial and natural), abortion, infanticide, and corruption. To join the rest of us, children must successfully run a homicidal gauntlet, and when they *do* make it, they are then turned over to governmental indoctrination centers so that they can acquire our widespread cultural loathing of fruitfulness.

This indoctrination takes many forms, but one obvious example is the near-universal presence of certain doctrines in the government schools. Take, for example, this one: "Thou shalt not overpopulate the earth." This secular doctrine is overtly promoted and presented as neutral ecological truth, when it is actually a challenge to the cultural mandate that God gave us in Genesis 1:28. The result is that the church is filled with people, educated at government schools, who feel at some level that it is a sin to have more than 1.7 children. But this is not biblical thinking at all. Obededom gloried in his eight sons, "for God blessed him" (1 Chron. 26:5). The world is not overpopulated. But the secular propaganda machine tells us that every new baby is just another mouth to feed and that we are all careening toward global starvation. They use this lie to argue that abortion is a more compassionate option than birth.

We are born with one mouth and two hands, and as we learn to live under the blessing of God, we will produce more than we consume. But if we disobey God, we will come to consume more than we produce, and we will indeed have too many *disobedient* people around. But this state of affairs results from disregarding God's Word, and we must always remember that God teaches us that a large population is a nation's glory. "In the multitude of people is the king's honour: but in the want of people is the destruction of the prince" (Prov. 14:28, KJV). Many Christians blindly accept the idea of the world's overpopulated status because this is the way they were educated. The Bible teaches something very different.

Unnatural Passions

Another judgment is homosexuality, which, of course, is another form of fruitlessness. The current homosexual agenda is very much at the center of government schools. Those involved in various forms of "gay pride," heavily promoted in sex education courses, want to pretend that they are refusing to do the will of God. But they are refusing to obey the commands of God because God already has judged them and given them up to such behavior:

> ✗ Therefore *God also gave them up* to uncleanness, in the lusts of their hearts, to dishonor their bodies among themselves . . . For this reason *God gave them up* to vile passions. For even their women exchanged the natural use for what is against nature. Likewise also the men, leaving the natural use of the woman, burned in their lust for one another, men with men committing what is shameful, and receiving in themselves the penalty of their error which was due (Rom. 1:24–27). ✗

Homosexuality is not only something that brings judgment from God. Homosexuality itself *is* a judgment from God. But the debates over this issue in the school system reveal how unbiblical many reforming Christians are as they express their concerns. For example, suppose that the issue of hiring homosexual teachers arises. Involved Christians may try to prove that homosexual teachers are more likely to molest children than heterosexual teachers. The debate then becomes statistical with competing graphs, charts, research studies, and so forth.

But these parents have been completely outmaneuvered. By making this argument, they are saying that they would be perfectly content with a homosexual teacher if he left their children alone sexually. Then it is perfectly acceptable for that teacher to be set up as an admirable role model, molesting their little hearts and minds. By how they frame the debate, such parents have made it possible for their opponents to show that homosexual teachers are not more likely to molest the children, thus silencing their opposition.

This approach is an utterly unbiblical way to proceed. We do not establish our ethical system on the basis of sociological research, but rather on the basis of the Word of God. Christian parents have a duty before God to protect their children in everything. The central duty they have before God is to protect the *minds* of their children. But the way many Christian parents fight the "culture wars" at their child's school shows that this duty has fallen by the wayside.

Crimes and Misdemeanors

Another divine judgment is crime. Many thousands of students have to pass through *metal detectors* in order to attend class. What is wrong with this picture?

The Bible says that where judgment is not speedily executed, the heart of man is fully set to do evil (Eccles. 8:11). Do we see this process at work in our government schools? Harmony within a citizenry is a gift of God. But when we are set against one another, this is the judgment of God. "For I set all men, everyone, against his neighbor" (Zech. 8:10). Christian children are not endangered because of some impersonal process. They are endangered because for generations we have been given over to judicial blindness and all the consequences that flow from such blindness.

Stupid Laws and Slap Suits

God also brings judgment through stupid laws. One of God's great instruments as He governs the world is His practice of <u>blinding the "wise."</u> The prophet says that it was "because they had not executed My judgments, but had despised My statutes, profaned My Sabbaths, and their eyes were fixed on their fathers' idols. Therefore I also gave them up to statutes that were not good, and judgments by which they could not live" (Ezek. 20:24–25).

The system of education we have in this country is *unworkable.* Why do we keep trying to make it work? The answer is that God has turned us over to our folly. He is the one who gives us statutes that are not good (forced bussing, whole language instruction, Outcome-Based Education, sex education for tots, *ad infinitum*). We complain under these judgments, but complaining is not the same as repentance.

Sometimes we sue, which brings us to a related sign of judgment—an abundance of lawsuits. The United States has 6 percent of the world's population and 70 percent of its lawyers. The prophets predict, "They have spoken words, swearing falsely in making a covenant. Thus judgment springs up like hemlock in the furrows of the field" (Hos. 10:4). The word *judgment* here refers to lawsuits, and hemlock is a poisonous plant. The unbelievers in our midst believe in salvation through litigation, and too many professing Christians have followed them in this particular idolatry. Christ is our Savior, and no other. So why do we look to the circuit judge?

Multiculturalism

Another judgment is more apparent in some parts of our country than others, but it is a significant judgment on our school system overall. We must come to see *destructive* immigration as being a clear judgment from God. "The alien who is among you shall rise higher and higher above you, and you shall come down lower and lower. He shall lend to you, but you shall not lend to him; he shall be the head, and you shall be the tail" (Deut. 28:43–44).

- The issue is not immigration in itself, but rather the *nature* of the immigration. Too often we act as though the issue were simply how many non-natives were coming across the border. The real concern is whether immigrants fear God. If they do, they bring blessing with them. But if they do not, they represent a striking judgment on us. -

This is the fallacy of multiculturalism in the curriculum of government schools today. This new emphasis does not represent a charitable attitude of tolerance, but an invading army of new gods. Tolerance, of course, is the initial demand, but the demand immediately following is that any system of faith *except Christianity* should be honored. We already find ourselves well down this road. Government schools can promote wellness, meditation, witchcraft, and tribal gods, just so long as they don't sing *Joy to the World* at that traditional "Winter Festival" we strange Westerners like to observe for some reason. -

The Fem Factor

- Connected to all these judgments is the fact of "missing men." We have lost the meaning of true masculine leadership in the home, the church, and the nation. This development too is from the hand of God:–

> I will give children to be their princes, and babes shall rule over them . . . As for My people, children are their oppressors, and women rule over them. O My people! Those who lead you cause you to err, and destroy the way of your paths (Isa. 3:4,12).

This loss of masculinity is both formal (a part of the curriculum) and informal with countless little acts of cowardice on the part of fathers. First, the formal inculcation of feminism as an article of faith in the government schools is beyond dispute. This is the formal adoption of a view of the sexual relation between man and woman that directly contradicts what the Bible says. When Christian parents have their children in government schools, what are those children learning about the relationships between the sexes?–Are the children taught that men and women are created by God to fulfill different roles, and that they each find their glory in assuming the station that God has assigned to them? Of course not! –

In countless ways, children are taught that the created differences between man and woman are actually social constructs, and unjust ones at that. Because we are accustomed to it, we doubt that this is happening in our schools. But a simple thought experiment should set the matter at rest. Just imagine what would happen during an accreditation visit with attentive reporters standing around if a second grade teacher made a point of telling the kids that all the girls there should be really looking forward to being mommies. The result would be the journalistic equivalent of a lynching.–The only reason we think that freedom of speech still exists is that everyone is well-trained, and we will only say what makes our masters happy. America is that *special* kind of free country where everyone does what they're told. –

This unrelenting feminist propaganda machine is reinforced by a general abdication of true masculinity, primarily in the home. Fathers have refused to act the part of *fathers* as the minds of their children are routinely and systematically molested. By the thousands, fathers act as though this mental molestation is not happening. This denial only adds to the problem.

A Reason for Hope

Those under the judgments we have discussed have not yet come to see them for what they really are. Occasionally, they recognize what they perceive to be a "problem" of some sort, big enough to complain about, maybe even big enough for a letter to the editor or to their congressman. But the problem is not so big that it must be confronted and dealt with. "My people love to have it so. But what will you do in the end? . . . They have also healed the hurt of My people slightly, saying, 'Peace, peace!' when there is no peace" (Jer. 5:31; 6:14).

Nevertheless, there is reason for hope. Although 2 Chronicles 7:14 has been greatly mishandled in the past, there is still hope contained within it.

> If My people who are called by My name will humble themselves, and pray and seek My face, and turn from their wicked ways, then I will hear from heaven, and will forgive their sin and heal their land (2 Chron. 7:14).

God loves to forgive the repentant, and the fact that we have been brought to the point where some of us can even see these things is cause for great hope. For the sake of our risen Lord and empowered by the Spirit, we must walk in obedience by repenting—by turning from our sin and rebellion against Him and embracing Him as our only hope in this life and the life to come.

"Turning to the Lord is one thing," you say, "but giving my children a distinctively Christian education is quite another. I came out with my faith still intact, so what could be so wrong about it? What about the cost? What about special-needs children? What about sports programs?" These and other good questions always arise in discussions about Christian education. The next chapter focuses on each of them.

12

OBJECTIONS
OVERRULED

*"There is little hope for children who are educated wickedly.
If the dye has been in the wool, it is hard to get it out of the cloth."*
—JEREMIAH BURROUGHS

In arguing that Christian parents are called by God to give their children a distinctively Christian education, I am not suggesting that parents who leave their children in government schools do not have their reasons. They may have many reasons for the choice they have made. The point of this chapter is to address some of the more common among them.

 Why shouldn't I let my children attend the public schools? I went through the public school system, and I turned out all right. The short answer to this objection is that parents who make this assertion didn't turn out all right. Believing that our experience in public education validates our children's education reveals that the standard for making this determination is found in man's wisdom, not God's. The biblical response is that we should look to the Word of God for direction, not our own lives. Our lives do not provide the standard. In the kindness of God, our lives may provide examples of faithfulness to the revealed standard, but our experience does not establish our duties.

The parent who believes that because government schools were good enough for him they must be good enough for his kids is obviously looking to something other than the Bible for his standard. The horrible irony is that he thinks this way precisely because he was educated by government schools to think this way. Man is not the standard. Second Corinthians 10:12 warns us that those who are "measuring themselves by themselves, and comparing themselves among themselves, are not wise." God is the standard and has revealed His standard in the Bible.

Christian schools are expensive. We cannot afford the tuition. This objection points to a very real problem. Christian schools cost money, and those parents who enroll their children there are paying for two school systems: one through their taxes, and the other through tuition. But we must understand the problem accurately and in its proper context.

If providing a Christian education is a moral obligation, somehow parents must bear the costs associated with that moral obligation. Food is expensive also, but no one argues that we should not feed our children. It is a given that we are morally required to feed our kids.

Parents first should study the Scriptures to find out if a Christian education is an obligation. If it is, then they should go before the Lord to seek *His* provision for their children. I do not want to sound cavalier; I write as someone who is sympathetic. My wife and I provided three children with an education that we could not "afford," and I am not really sure how we did it. God was kind to us, but this sort of thing requires sacrifice over the long haul, and there is no substitute that makes it easy. The one thing that makes it possible is the conviction that God requires it.

God's Word promises that "He will supply all your need according to His riches in glory by Christ Jesus" (Phil. 4:19). Just as God uses the church to help some families provide food for their children, so He can use the church to help some families provide a Christian education for their children. Perhaps the school can offer scholarships to less fortunate students. Or perhaps the church can do so, either officially through the support of the deacons or unofficially through more fortunate families sponsoring those less fortunate. And if parents feel called by God to do so, they can always homeschool, an inexpensive option for many families who want to obey God for the sake of their children.

86

We distinguish between the physical realm of creation and the spiritual realm of redemption and believe that education is primarily within the realm of creation, not redemption. Therefore, the Bible does not really require a formal Christian education as long as we do our job at home and at church. Separating the "realm of redemption" and the "realm of creation" does not leave us with anything to be redeemed. The creation is still lost, and the realm of redemption is empty.

The issue is simply this: In the Great Commission, Jesus Christ said that all authority in heaven *and on earth* was given to Him (Matt. 28:18). This was His basis for sending us out to disciple the nations. He did not say that all authority in the realm of redemption was given to Him and that the realm of creation operated under some other authority. Jesus Christ has been given the name that is above every name, whether in heaven, on earth, or under the earth.

To take this truth as meaning only that His name is above every name in just a "spiritual sense" is ultimately to introduce a gnostic dualism into our Christian faith, holding that the material is bad, if not inferior, while the spiritual is good or superior. If we take this plunge, the consequences are not small—as witnessed by children of Christians being taught by someone other than Jesus Christ how to think about creation.

They are taught this because it is assumed that Christ does not have authority in the realm of creation. It is a small step from this thinking for the children to assume that Christ does not have authority over created things—which is to deny who He is.

My child is different and is ready for government schools. This objection might be valid, depending on the child. In other words, if it could be lawful for a young person to attend a secular university (13th grade), then why is it magically unlawful for them to attend a secular high school (12th grade)?

Obviously, the Bible does not teach us that we cannot talk to unbelievers or that we cannot listen to them when they speak. Nor are we required to stay away from books they have written. No such restrictions are placed on our children either.

At the same time, it is not right for our children to be educated by unbelievers. Scriptures require us to see to it that our children have a Christian education. If this has been done and the "concrete is hard"—if the child can take a class from an unbeliever and can sort out the worldview issues—then there is no problem. If a child has been equipped with armor and weapons, there is nothing wrong with sending him to war.

But of course, most Christian young people are not ready for a secular university, and as we descend to the lower grades, they are decreasingly ready. Third graders cannot identify what is being done to them, while a few significantly older kids (if they have been rigorously educated in a Christian worldview) might be able to stand their ground.

The principle is this: If a child has already received a thorough and complete Christian education, then it is certainly lawful for him to hear what unbelievers have to say. If he has not, then what he hears from unbelievers will be his education, and the parents who allowed this to happen have been disobedient.

Our local Christian school has a weak competitive athletic program. Our family believes that athletic competition is very important. The subject of athletics is a complicated one, so we have to talk about sports in general before talking about the role of sports in deciding whether a child should receive a distinctively Christian education. That athletics is far too important to many families is evident in the simple fact that it is used to justify disobedience to God in how our children are educated.

When a ball is involved, emotions easily run high. Some Christian parents get fired up in behalf of their Little Leaguers, while others get spiritually stressed out at the very thought of competition. Once that issue is addressed, we can then evaluate how important it is for our children to participate in sports.

The first question concerns the lawfulness of athletic competition: Is it right or wrong in itself? We must never forget that the Bible alone determines the boundaries of sin. Not once does Scripture hint that athletic competition should be considered as immoral or sinful. The Bible determines the definition of sin, not the traditions of men.—We have no more ground for saying that athletic competition is sinful than we have for saying that blue curtains are sinful.—The defender of athletics does not have to prove from Scripture that such competition is lawful; he must simply show that Scripture does not prohibit it, either explicitly or implicitly. If God had wanted His children to stay away from balls in motion, He would have said so.

With this understanding, we can then consider how the common athletic metaphors in Scripture speak to the issue of sports.—Paul, for example, uses many such metaphors, as in his first epistle to the Corinthians:

> Do you not know that those who run in a race all run, but one receives the prize? Run in such a way that you may obtain it. And everyone who competes for the prize is temperate in all things. Now they do it to obtain a perishable crown, but we for an imperishable crown. Therefore I run thus: not with uncertainty. Thus I fight: not as one who beats the air. But I discipline my body and bring it into subjection, lest, when I have preached to others, I myself should become disqualified (1 Cor. 9:24–27). —

This passage does not tell us to attract unbelievers to the faith with the persistence of a serial murderer, but of a runner. Paul obviously appeals to an ordinary and lawful part of human life to teach us about the Christian life.

Too many Christians, however, assume that once the lawfulness of an activity has been established, we are free to pursue it the same way the world does. But the world has enough power to place all kinds of hooks in lawful bait—and it does. Athletic competition is one of the few things that government schools still do well, and they generally surpass Christian schools in this area. Many parents allow their children to attend government schools for precisely this reason.

So suppose that parents have their child at the government school because of the sports program. More is involved in this decision than simply receiving a college scholarship. The central problem is that such parents have adopted an anti-biblical mindset. The pursuit of a *ball* is more important to them than the pursuit of *wisdom.* I have been very grateful for the opportunity my kids had to pursue "the ball," but if I had permitted them to pursue the ball instead of pursuing the fear of the Lord, I would have been guilty of gross parental negligence.

There are lesser problems as well. One of them, depending on the sport, is that we have somehow assumed that the interests of speed, or some other function of athletic performance, set aside the requirements of propriety and modesty. In the ancient world, athletes competed naked. In the modern world in some events, they might as well be. One question that may come to mind during a competition is, "Where is that girl's mother?"

We can tell that "athletics" has become a false religion because it has begun to dictate behavioral norms that contradict what the Bible says. Christians are to be modest, and if that slows them down, tough. But Christians who compete in government schools rarely do anything other than "fit in."

Another problem, as Paul's use of sports imagery attests, comes from the fact that the world of athletics is rich with didactic images. We should not be surprised that the world rushes to teach false doctrine through athletics. For example, one doctrine athletics inculcates is that of feminism, and in government schools, Christian parents are required not to make any compromises on this point. Parents who allow their girls to participate in athletics must insist that their daughters never forget their femininity for a moment. They also must not allow their daughters to participate in events that are inherently masculine or to participate in a program that does not adequately distinguish between boys and girls.

Boys should learn to compete like men. Girls should learn to compete like ladies. To take an obvious example, girls should not wrestle or play football. In contrast, the differing rules between men's and women's lacrosse honor God. If we understand how God made us, we should look for distinctions between male and female versions of the same point, not a blurring of those distinctions. But in modern government schools, blurring those distinctions is a high priority.

Of course, another false doctrine is that of self-worship. Interviews after athletic competitions reveal scores of athletes who have learned their catechism well. "I discovered that I could only get here by reaching down and believing in myself." To which the Christian should be able to respond, "Pish. And tosh." Nothing is neutral. Parents are to instruct their children to live as believing Christians when they rise up, lie down, walk along the way, and run the bases. This means staying away from government schools.

Finally, numerous youth sports programs are available. Many Christian schools offer such programs, as do parks and private leagues. Our children can participate in sports without attending government schools.

My kids have had an unbelieving piano teacher and have had unbelieving Little League coaches, so what's the difference between that and attending government schools? The difference between these situations is the difference between an hour a week, accompanied by a parent, and seven hours a day, unaccompanied by a parent. The objection is kind of like wondering why a child can play in the surf when his parents won't let him swim a mile off shore.

The point made in this book is not that non-Christians have cooties. Rather, the point is that parents are responsible for how a child learns and what he learns. If parents know that no damaging lessons are being learned from the non-Christian piano teacher, then they have not abdicated anything. They are in control of the lessons—which is not the case in the government schools. But note that this control must be exercised, even with piano teachers or Little League coaches. Many wise parents have changed piano teachers or Little League coaches for just this reason. When they do, they have the authority and the knowledge to make a right decision.

One of my children is academically advanced and the other is a special needs student. No Christian school in our area can meet their needs. This is an important issue, and I am reluctant to answer it too briefly lest I appear glib about a problem that is heartrending to many parents.

First, an observation. In most cases, children with special needs are _more vulnerable_ in government schools, not less. Consequently, it is more important to get them what they need in the way of Christian education, not less important.

For the academically advanced child, a good Christian school is very important so that he does not come to believe that the life of the mind and the life of the soul are two different things. He needs to be challenged at every level, and this is much more likely in a good Christian school than in a government school.

For the special needs child, there are two possible categories of children. First, we must recognize that an entire class of "special needs children" has been created by the government school system. Children with dyslexia, attention deficit syndrome, and so forth are frequently children who have not been taught or disciplined lovingly or wisely in the light of a Christian worldview. If children in this category are kept in a government program to help them, they are being treated by those who probably made them sick in the first place.

Of course, there are true special needs children who are not created by the government school system, and this situation calls for special sensitivity. The children may be blind, or have cerebral palsy, or mild Downs syndrome.

In such cases, I would suggest to parents that they address the educational needs of their child on the same principles that they use when making decisions about their children's medical treatment. This might mean moving to an urban area, where cooperation with other Christian parents in the same situation becomes feasible. If the population base is large enough, it might mean starting a Christian school with a special needs program. If the parents live in a rural area and moving is not an option, it might mean starting a distance-learning homeschooling cooperative, utilizing the Internet.

⌐The basic principle is this: Families who embrace their responsibilities in the realm of education, regardless of their circumstances, can look for the blessing of God, as well as the help of the other saints. ⌐

My kids think that the kids at the Christian school are simply "out of it." They do not want to go to such an uncool place.-Parents are fighting that great enemy of the faith called "cool."-No one knows exactly the nature of this enemy.

Whenever they hear some appeal to a standard, Christian parents should immediately ask whether that standard is biblical.-The standard of *cool* certainly is not, and fortunately, neither is the standard of nerdiness found at many Christian schools. The fact that a child is appealing to such a standard reveals the screaming need that child has for a Christian education.- He wants to go to government schools because he is thinking like an unbeliever and wants to go where many others do the same.

To illustrate, let's take an example of the weird adornment that is so appealing on kids at government schools. And let's assume that the Christian kids want to get over there and be like that. So what do Christian parents do when their eldest son wants an eyebrow ring? Generally, when these things happen, parents don't have any problem going sideways in some fashion, but they usually do so on the basis of some traditional value or other. The disintegration of the culture we see around us, however, should have taught us long ago that our traditional values are really nothing but a mud fence built to withstand a tidal wave.

The first issue to consider is the necessity of a good teaching relationship between parents and teenagers. Too often we define "good relationship" as one in which no one is yelling, and we leave out one of the things which God says characterizes a good relationship.-"My son, hear the *instruction* of thy father, and forsake not the *law* of thy mother" (Prov. 1:8, KJV).-This is why parents must have a biblical worldview, because if they do not, then the children certainly will not.

So suppose such a "good" relationship has been established, but the parents do not know what to say to their child. They assume the reason for their dislike of "the earring" is related to their being terminally unhip.-When their teenager wants to fit in with the other kids, they do not feel as though they have any biblical basis for saying no.-And if they were to say *no*, they do not know how they would justify it scripturally. To confess the need to learn how to do this is to confess the need our children have for the kind of education we did not receive. Instead, parents must help their children live biblical lives and they must ensure that they receive a distinctively Christian education so they can make such decisions for themselves and their own children one day.

My children are mine. No one should tell me how to raise them or what kind of education is best for them. The answer here is twofold. First, our children are ours in the sense that they have been entrusted to us as stewards. But as stewards, we will give an accounting to the One who entrusted them to us. — The children of Christians belong to the Lord; they are His. If this is the case and if He has instructed us on how He wants them educated, then the matter is settled. Now if the claim is that God has not placed this requirement on us, then we must answer the arguments presented elsewhere in this book. But if the arguments are not answered, then the obligation to educate children before the Lord remains.

The second response is related to the first. As Christians, we are called by God to live together in community. This means that what my children do is not irrelevant to other families. We cannot adopt a rugged, individualistic approach. When a child is baptized in sound churches, the whole community of believers surrounding the family is also involved. They promise to pray for the parents as they bring up their children in the nurture and admonition of the Lord. Given this covenantal connection, it is not interference (if done with discretion and wisdom) to suggest to a brother and friend that he might want to consider the biblical basis of a Christian education for his children.

What you are saying about children in the government schools makes sense. But what about Christian teachers employed by the government school system? This is an entirely different problem. Given the principles outlined in earlier chapters, an adult Christian with a settled worldview in place can certainly teach in government schools without sinning. But he cannot teach there without frustration.

However, he may find that, in order to keep his job, receive favorable treatment, or advance in his career, he is tempted to compromise. The curriculum is often dictated from on high, and there just is no way to teach an ungodly worldview from a Christian perspective.

He is in a quandary. If he has a Christian influence on the kids or on the institution, then he is going to come into conflict with the system. If he has no such influence, then no conflict occurs except inside himself.

The reason he teaches is to have a positive impact on kids. For a Christian to teach without shining the light of the gospel through his daily activities turns his job into a simple matter of teaching for money. But for good teachers, this is inadequate and ultimately unsatisfying.

Put simply, the teacher can make a difference or not. If he makes a difference, his case will probably appear before the Supreme Court. If he is not making a difference, then why not go where he can?

So far, we have seen that God calls Christians to provide a distinctively Christian education for their children. But Christians also need to understand what is involved in such an education. We turn now to explore exactly how to teach our children *well*.

13
TEACH YOUR CHILDREN WELL

✕ *"When, in the 1890s, the classical curriculum tried to compete with the sciences by becoming 'scientific' too, it signed its own death warrant."* ✕
—*JACQUES BARZUN*

We have seen that Christian parents, especially fathers, are commanded to bring up their children in the *education* of the Lord, to give them a distinctively Christian education. But what specifically does that mean? Of the various forms of Christian education available, what does Scripture require of us?

Features of True Christian Education

To answer these questions, we turn to Psalm 78:1–11 for guidance:

> Give ear, O my people, to my law; incline your ears to the words of my mouth. I will open my mouth in a parable; I will utter dark sayings of old, which we have heard and known, and our fathers have told us. We will not hide them from their children, telling to the generation to come the praises of the LORD, and His strength and His wonderful works that He has done. For He established a testimony in Jacob, and appointed a law in Israel, which He commanded our fathers, that they should make them known to their children; that the generation to come might know them, the children who would be born, that they may arise and declare them to their children, that they may set their

> hope in God, and not forget the works of God, but keep His commandments; and may not be like their fathers, a stubborn and rebellious generation, a generation that did not set its heart aright, and whose spirit was not faithful to God. The children of Ephraim, being armed and carrying bows, turned back in the day of battle. They did not keep the covenant of God; they refused to walk in His law, and forgot His works and His wonders that He had shown them.

In this text, we see a number of essential features of true Christian education. One is that such education is God-centered. The psalmist tells us in verse 4 that we are to tell our children the praises of the *Lord* and the wonderful things that *He* has done. In verse 7, we see that failure in this regard meant that they forgot the works of God. If we educate our children without any reference to God, what are we doing except actively teaching them to do what this psalm forbids? What are we doing but showing our children how to *forget* what God told us to have them remember?

In 1776, the fathers of our country declared their independence from Great Britain and fought the Revolutionary War. Things in the government school system have gotten so bad that they frequently don't even teach students the "raw" information about that war. Modern students are quite frankly historically disoriented. But even in the "good schools," where the students learn that we did separate from Great Britain in the eighteenth century, what do they learn about what *God* did for us in that conflict?

A student in the government schools is lucky if he learns that the war had something to do with a tax on tea. But that was a small part of the conflict. The single biggest controversy before the war involved whether or not the king was going to appoint an Anglican archbishop over all thirteen colonies.

More than half the soldiers in the Continental army were Presbyterians. At Yorktown, all of Washington's colonels, with one exception, were elders in the Presbyterian Church. In Britain, one of the names of the war was the "Presbyterian revolt." Taking a jibe at Witherspoon, who was a signer of the

Declaration of Independence, one English colonist said that cousin America had run off with a Presbyterian parson. Presbyterian pastors, because of their black Geneva gowns and their support of the war, were known as the black regiment. Just as other wars have had rallying cries ("Remember Pearl Harbor"), so did the War for Independence—"No king but King Jesus!"

Our psalm tells us that we are responsible to tell our children about the mighty works of God in the history of His people. This is something we have refused to do. In addition to this failure, many Christian parents continue to have their children enrolled in schools where it is *illegal* to give glory to God for something God has done for us.

Moral Guidance

We also see in Psalm 78 that a truly Christian education provides the goal of moral direction. God has not left us in this world without moral orientation. In verse 5 of the psalm, He tells us that He established a "testimony in Jacob, and appointed a law in Israel." In verse 7, we see that an important part of teaching our children is to enable them to keep God's commandments.

The obligation to "be moral" is not something that can be sustained in mid-air. It does not matter how much the children in government schools are harangued about adopting "core values." If students are given no good reason to do so, they will not. We tell them, for example, not to smoke cigarettes. There has been quite a national ruckus about all this. But why not smoke?

They have been taught that they are nothing but the end result of millions of years of blind, random mutations and that they are nothing but a skin full of protoplasm. And then, for some mysterious reason, the authorities are appalled when the kids start acting just like what we have taught them they are—ultimately meaningless (when all is said and done). Why shouldn't a skin full of protoplasm get lung cancer?

When we look at some poor, sullen kid standing on the street corner with his tongue ring, purple hair, filthy shirt, tattoes and chains, we must not think for a moment that he is being rebellious. On the contrary, he is a most submissive student. He has apparently learned all of his lessons. LOL

The Grace of God

Genuine education also depends upon the grace of God. The psalm we are considering is quoted in Matthew 13:35. As we compare this quotation with the teaching in verses 11–13 of the same chapter, we can see that Christian education is a blessing of the covenant.

Parents who withhold Christian education are withholding one of their children's covenant privileges; they are withholding one of the means of grace—applying the Word to all of life. *Talk* about grace is insufficient; present grace is needed. This means that when living grace is present, the blessing is broken open and the people of God may eat.

When grace is not present, even though the language of grace is present, then those who are called by the name of God get all those covenant God-words wrapped around their necks. Wonderful words become dark parables. This is why nominal "Christian" education is worse than ungodly government education. But assuming that one must choose between these two is a false dilemma. Christian parents should turn away from overt unbelief in the education of their children, and they should just as resolutely turn away from a "Christian" education that mouths all the words, but does not really say anything.

Equips for Battle

We must also see that true Christian education equips our children for battle. The children of Ephraim turned back from battle because they forgot God's works. They forgot His works because they had not been taught those words.

Refusal to educate your children in the Lord is covenant-breaking, which results in cowardice and more covenant-breaking. Sinful forgetfulness on the part of parents leads to more sinful forgetfulness on the part of their children. We are responsible to *remember* and will give an account to God for our forgetfulness and neglectfulness.

A Way of Life

Given what we have seen, Christian education must be considered as a way of life. In this process, Christian parents prepare their children to be able to prepare their children so that they in turn will be able to prepare their children.

⟵Prepare them for what? To glorify and enjoy God, live according to His law, walk in the light of His grace, and fight His enemies with a whole heart. This is the end and purpose of all true Christian education.⟵

But the understanding that this is a way of life is subject to two common problems. The first is neglect through laziness, where a sorry and truncated form of education is substituted for the whole. Laziness is hard to overcome, but at least it is simple to understand. The second is neglect through misunderstanding. In the hands of some, Christian education is like pie dough. The farther it is spread, the thinner it gets. The false assumption undergirding this approach is that since everything should be part of Christian education, then everything we do must be Christian education. In a poor homeschooling setting, some may be tempted to call a jaunt to McDonalds a field trip. In a poor Christian school, a teacher assumes that if he stands in front of a class talking, the work of Christian education must be getting done. But true education involves constant, diligent *work*. The assumption of "automatic education" is a deadly one.

The Path Ahead

In the kindness of God today, we do see some indications that a measure of repentance has been given. But even in the best scenario, we are only in the initial stages of an educational reformation. What issues still lie before us?

The greatest one, and the central topic of this book, is the problem of government schools. While we should not be surprised that non-Christians support government schools, what should astonish us is the fact that the majority of professing Christians still seek to have their children shaped by the institutions of a rival religion. We can understand why the priests of Baal worship their god, but why do we do it?

We must be constantly vigilant. As more and more parents join the exodus from government schools, we must be wary of all forms of feigned reformation or partial solutions. Some folks always seem ready to throw their hats into the air for the next parade. But when the hard work arrives, which is necessary over an extended period of time, the story is frequently quite altered. A movement that does not discipline will not be a movement very long. This truism most certainly includes attempts by Christians to restore the true pattern of covenant education. But lest we be overwhelmed, we may look to the grace of God, who promises to mature His people (Eph. 4:11–16). And He will do so.

Classical Education

Some readers may be aware of the strong movement toward what is being called *classical* and Christian education.

What does classical education have to do with the Christian faith? As Tertullian once asked, "What does Jerusalem have to do with Athens?" Should we not just dismiss this question as a "secular" pedagogical issue? We cannot if we understand what it means to approach all things, education included, in the light of Scripture.

In a broader sense, all Christian education must be classical. There is a narrow use of the word that is not necessary to Christian education, although very helpful. Those interested in exploring this more restrictive sense can pursue the subject at length in my book *Recovering the Lost Tools of Learning*.

The broad outlines of the classical methodology are assumed in Scripture. "The fear of the LORD is the beginning of knowledge, but fools despise wisdom and instruction" (Prov. 1:7). This point is where we must always start. All things must begin with a healthy fear of God. If we begin with ourselves or with ancient men, we will always stumble and fall. If we do not base everything we do on the teaching of Scripture, that compromise, at some point, will undo us.

But the broad outlines of the classical methodology certainly can be found in Scripture. How so? As my friend Randy Booth has helpfully pointed out, the Bible makes a distinction between various forms of "knowing," as illustrated in this passage from Proverbs. They are *knowledge*, *understanding*, and *wisdom*. Throughout Scripture, we regularly see them distinguished, sometimes in the same passage: "For the LORD gives wisdom; from His mouth come knowledge and understanding" (Prov. 2:6; cf. Exod. 35:34). As we will now explore, the similarities between these distinctions and the classical terminology are so remarkable that it is clear that we are talking about the same basic things.

The Trivium

Private classical Christian schools use the terminology of the trivium, where the pattern of learning is divided into three stages: grammar, dialectic, and rhetoric. These schools also emphasize Latin, the fine arts, the study of formal rhetoric, and so forth. The cultural trappings of such classical schools are not necessary for all Christian schools. But the basic outline is required, and this outline is notably missing from all government schools.

What is meant by grammar, dialectic, and rhetoric is very similar to what Scripture intends with the words knowledge, understanding, and wisdom. We first see the parallel between knowledge and grammar. "Cease listening to instruction, my son, and you will stray from the words of knowledge" (Prov. 19:27). In Scripture, *knowledge* is connected with hearing (or refusing to hear) very specific words of instruction. A fool does not want to be bothered. One who is diligent to hear will come to wisdom. In the classical method, *grammar* refers to the body of information which must be taken in by the student and which is given at the beginning of his course of instruction.

Second, we turn to the comparison between understanding and dialectic. "The fear of the LORD is the beginning of wisdom; a good understanding have all those who do His commandments" (Ps. 111:10). In Scripture, *understanding* has a strong ethical component, A scriptural approach to ethics emphasizes discernment—*this*, not *that*. In the classical method, dialectic refers to the practice of sorting out and relating all the knowledge that has been and is being accumulated. "This goes here, and that goes there." All Christian educators must acknowledge that *clear thinking is a moral issue.* Being a clothhead is a sin. To teach the dialectical stage without a constant grounding in the ethical absolutes of Scripture is worse than folly.

Third, we see the connection between wisdom and rhetoric. "The tongue of the wise uses knowledge rightly, but the mouth of fools pours forth foolishness" (Prov. 15:2). In Scripture, *wisdom* refers to the arrangement and application of knowledge and understanding. The ability to do this will lead to more knowledge and understanding, which will in turn be arranged appropriately. Wisdom answers the question of how to present or apply knowledge. Not surprisingly, in the classical method, rhetoric assumes essentially the same role. Someone who was "good" at rhetoric was not a person who was quick with words. Given the number of law schools in our country, our modern rejection of rhetoric as sophistry—false and deceptive argument—is understandable (and Socrates felt the same way), but this definition is at odds with some of the best classical meanings of rhetoric. Just as a man cannot be wise without being good, so a man cannot be a rhetorician in the biblical sense without being good.

One can claim that a school can get along without using the classical definitions of grammar, dialectic, and rhetoric. But what Christian parent will say that knowledge, understanding, and wisdom are optional? Asked this way, the answer is obvious. However, we have to be reminded that all parents who have their kids in government schools *are* saying that these things are optional.

The Historical Context

The other important feature of classical and Christian education has to do with the content of what is taught. Other forms of Christian education should emphasize this aspect as well. Why do we emphasize the history of western civilization? Why does the content matter? Unless this question is answered biblically, Christian parents will have no defense against the onslaught of multiculturalism.

We must have a doctrine of history. In the providence of God, the kingdom of God was preached in the Greco-Roman world and spread, for the most part, north and west. This has changed only in the last century or so. Of course, the kingdom of God *is not to be identified with western culture*, but the stories of each are so intertwined that we cannot hope to understand the course of one without knowing the history of the other. As Christian educators, this means that Constantine and Charlemagne will always be more significant to us than the Ming Dynasty. But in government schools, events that were insignificant to our development as a people are strongly emphasized. This is not an expression of cultural charity; the tactic is a battering ram, designed not to teach appreciation for other cultures, but rather contempt for our own.

Our children are not interchangeable ball-bearings, able to be placed in any number of machines around the world; they are olive shoots around our *own* tables. So we must have a doctrine of generations that allows our children to *grow*. They do not grow up in a detached way, as though the twig were unrelated to the branch, which, in turn, is unrelated to the tree.

The problem we encounter is that we think of previous generations or eras as a series of small duck ponds. We used to live around a pond that everyone called "the fifties." Later, we lived around another pond called "the nineties."

But this is not how the Bible encourages us to think about history at all. History is a river, and we live downstream from our ancestors and upstream from our descendants. Learning to think this way is a return to the biblical mind, and it necessarily involves Caesar Augustus, Charles Martel, John Calvin, and Robert E. Lee.

As we come to understand why Christian children need a Christian education and learn the hallmarks of all true Christian education, we also need to avoid some of the pitfalls of Christian education, whether in traditional schools or in homeschools. We turn next to some of those pitfalls.

14
PITFALLS TO AVOID

✗   *"True education is, in a sense, a spiritual process, the nurture of a soul . . .
Every line of true knowledge must find its completeness in its convergency to God,
even as every beam of daylight leads the eye to the sun. If religion be excluded
from our study, every process of thought will be arrested before it reaches its
proper goal . . . A non-Christian training is literally an anti-Christian training."* ✗
—R. L. DABNEY

Parents who pull their children out of government schools simply in reaction to the latest outrage usually end up building Christian schools or homeschools that are not rigorously Christian.-The Christian school is not just a substitute for the government school down the street.-It is a different *kind* of school altogether. The same goes for homeschooling; the homeschool cannot be a small version of what government schools accomplish. Regardless of whether they use a private school or a homeschool as their method of choice, Christian parents must provide an alternative to governmental groupthink. Of course, while both homeschools and traditional Christian schools present unique problems, they have enough in common for all Christian parents to profit from the warnings for each. So in this chapter, I want to deliver a series of warnings regarding the pitfalls to avoid, whether in Christian schools or in Christian homeschools.

Warnings for Christian Schools

Christian parents must be aware of the pitfalls often associated with Christian schools.

Cheap Talk. God gives covenant promises that overarch the task of all true education.

> The mercy of the LORD is from everlasting to everlasting on those who fear Him, and His righteousness to children's children, to such as keep His covenant, and to those who remember His commandments to do them (Ps. 103:17–18).

This means the parents are not to provide a Christian education for the kids because it "seems like a good idea" to someone. They are to provide this kind of education because they are *keeping covenant* and because they fear God and *remember His commandments*. In doing this by faith, they are looking for everlasting mercy, not justice, so that the righteousness of our Lord Jesus Christ will flow over all their descendents. That is why they make the sacrifice.

Certain principles should be in the forefront in the minds of parents who undertake this task. They should make sure that they do more than just talk. It is far easier to learn the jargon than to do what needs to be done. For example, someone might say, "Well, just because others are teaching my kids, that doesn't mean that I am not responsible . . ." This is quite right, but only for those parents who *understand* it. Scripture tells us that the *father* must be educating his children by means of a school: "And you, fathers, do not provoke your children to wrath, but bring them up in the training and admonition of the Lord" (Eph. 6:4).

The godly father should not get someone else to do it for him. Put simply, parents who enroll their children in a private Christian school (regardless of how good the school is), and then walk away or fail to get involved in their children's education, are disobedient parents. On the other hand, parents who use a good Christian school as a tool in the way they educate their children are, by His grace, doing what He requires.

Self-Serving Factions. When parents go the route of Christian schools, they must learn to understand giving "in community." In an institution of any size, it is very natural (and very wrong) for certain "interest groups" to develop. One potential group consists of the teachers; another consists of parents; yet another, secondary students; still another, the administration; and so forth.

Tuition is an obvious issue around which political factions could develop self-interest. By Paul says, "Let each of you look out not only for his own interests, but also for the interests of others" (Phil. 2:4). In a worldly institution, parents watch out for parents, teachers for teachers, and so on. In a godly institution, parents watch out for teachers, teachers for parents, and the administration for teachers. You get the picture. In a Christian institution such as a Christian school, the individuals involved should think and act like Christians.

Catering to Boys and Girls. Another important issue is the differences between boys and girls. Two things are important to remember. First, masculinity in students is not always "institution-friendly" while femininity usually is. One of the most valuable things an institution provides a boy, however, is the gift of misunderstanding him. A boy who is really "understood" (usually by his mother) is worthless. A boy almost always needs more lumps on the head than he usually gets.

Second, with girls, the father must remember to *maintain his headship*. This keeps allegiance from drifting in good situations. ("Mr. Smith is *such* a good teacher . . . !") It also protects his daughter in difficult situations. A daughter should not take the same kind of hits that a son should take.

Testing the Spirits. In an institution, we must avoid certain actions as well. Parents must make sure that they do not believe everything they hear. Parents will hear all kinds of things around the dinner table about teachers, other students, and other families. When the parents have heard from their kid, they still do not have the entire picture. Consequently, they should not act as though they do.

Solomon tells us that "the first one to plead his cause seems right, until his neighbor comes and examines him" (Prov. 18:17). Therefore, a father should not phone a teacher assuming that he knows why his child flunked that test. He should phone, of course, but just to inquire. After he has heard everyone out, he has enough information to think and pray about the situation. He should not talk with his child, then get on the phone loaded for bear.

Peer Pressure. Parents also must not forget the power of peer pressure. School is a good place to learn how to live in community. And godly peer pressure is a wonderful thing. But in a fallen world, ungodly pressure exists as well, even in a school with sound discipline.

Parents should never *assume* that the school has the peer-pressure situation covered. Prepare your kids beforehand.—"My son, if sinners entice you, do not consent"—(Prov. 1:10). Learning to live in community is valuable; learning groupthink is useless, if not harmful.

Age Segregation. Parents should watch for ungodly age segregation. We should teach students according to their capacities and divide them into classrooms generally by age. Such division is not, as some claim, a manifestation of modernity. Dividing kids by their ages is as old as dirt.

But when the juniors think the sophomores should not be spoken to, and the freshmen think that when *they* are seniors things will be much improved, then there is a serious spiritual problem. Paul encourages us to "be of the same mind toward one another. Do not set your mind on high things, but associate with the humble. Do not be wise in your own opinion" (Rom. 12:16).

Using family ties is a wonderful way to deal with this problem. Nothing is more endearing than to see a boy in high school watching out for his sister in the sixth grade.

Haughty Spirits. In a good school, students are tempted with pride. While the Bible does not discourage satisfaction in a job done well, it does teach us that conceit is always contemptible. As Paul put it, "Let each one examine his own work, and then he will have rejoicing in himself alone, and not in another. For each one shall bear his own load" (Gal. 6:4–5). One kind of pride is lawful, and another is not. One of the greatest indications of a superior education is true humility.

If parents are excited about a wonderful Christian school they have found for their children, they might find it easy to judge others. While it is fine for them to share their enthusiasm for their school choice and to encourage other Christian parents to explore its benefits, they should be careful not to become judgmental if others make different choices. "Who are you to judge another's servant? To his own master he stands or falls. Indeed, he will be made to stand, for God is able to make him stand" (Rom. 14:4).

Warnings for Christian Homeschools

This leads to one of those differing educational choices, that of homeschooling. Too often, reactionary homeschooling simply settles for being unlike government schools. But this is not good enough.

Of course, instruction must occur in *every* godly home. Remember the principle in Deuteronomy 4:6–7, and tailor your home education after the Lord's admonition to teach your children to love Him with all their heart, soul, mind, and strength.

So all these warnings should be heard in the context of a job well done. None of what I have to say should be taken as saying that *no one* is doing what they ought to do, or that all those who homeschool are necessarily guilty of the problems listed below. *Far from it.* Nevertheless the warnings must be delivered, and they are not hypothetical.

Prickliness. The first is the problem of "prickliness." Americans have a long tradition of "rugged individualism," which certainly has its virtues. But it also can result in isolation from others who are called to help. We are designed by God to live in community, and this means that we must be involved in each other's lives.

To live in community in a profitable way, we must exhibit the attitudes required in Scripture. "Who is wise and understanding

111

among you? Let him show by good conduct that his works are done in the meekness of wisdom" (James 3:13). Accepting a word of rebuke or instruction is particularly difficult when our children are involved. Not all criticism is an attack, and not all disagreement is an attempt to offend.

False Spirituality. Another problem is false spirituality. Some advocate that this particular method of educating is the only real evidence of being "sold out" to true Christian living. Maybe, maybe not. There *are* homeschoolers (and Christian schoolers) who really are "more spiritual." They are the ones who don't think they are. Remember Paul's admonition: "Why do you judge your brother? Or why do you show contempt for your brother? For we shall all stand before the judgment seat of Christ" (Rom. 14:10).

God makes distinctions among the saints and apportions the rewards of His kingdom accordingly. But *being* superior in the kingdom and *feeling* superior are two different things. Christ did not discourage those who wanted to be great in the kingdom of God. In fact, He instructed us on how to go about it. Walking around with our noses in the air was not part of the program. He established that the one who wants to be great in the kingdom must become the servant—a true servant—of all.

As we strive for excellence in how we educate, we must remember that humility adorns excellence. One time my daughter was asked by a young boy if she went to a private Christian school. When she said yes, the young boy confidently stated that those who homeschool are better than those who do not. Making allowances for the young man's age and immaturity, we must conclude that thinking in such categories is spiritually dangerous. We must strive for the best for us and our children, and striving for the best includes striving for true practical humility.

Unaccountability. Homeschooling circles sometimes have little academic accountability. Parents must take care that they do not allow themselves to drift into a situation where they let necessary work go by the wayside. "We dare not class ourselves or compare ourselves with those who commend themselves. But they, measuring themselves by themselves, and comparing themselves among themselves, are not wise" (2 Cor. 10:12).

When a student starts to fall behind in a classroom, his problem is usually obvious fairly soon. But in an isolated homeschool setting, children can be left behind because accountability is sometimes not in place as it should be. Homeschooling parents must make sure they count the cost. A true education at home is not possible without consistent self-discipline; parents cannot just wing it. Accountability applies to both parents and kids. Don't call it homeschooling if the people involved are only at home merely sitting.

The Needs of Boys and Girls.–Another common problem is not being hard enough on the boys. Boys like to be lazy, and they like to be indulged.-Parents who love them must never let up on their discipline. As a general rule, men tend to be too hard on the boys and too soft on the girls. Mothers are the opposite— too soft on the boys and too hard on the girls. But in a homeschool setting, when a boy is being educated primarily by his mother, the situation can create a series of difficult temptations. "My son, keep your father's command, and do not forsake the law of your mother" (Prov. 6:20). Boys need to be "knocked down" a few times during childhood, and they usually need to get it harder than a mother is willing to deliver it.

At the same time, girls should never be forgotten in the process of education. Many times families who choose to homeschool are also families with a large number of kids. Learning to cook and take care of younger children is only a *portion* of home education. The most difficult time in educating must come at just the time when the students would be a tremendous help around the house with the little ones. Homeschooling for daughters can drift into something else altogether. Parents should not let this happen.

Shyness and Overconfidence. Then there is the problem of "socialization." To judge from the amount of space devoted to answering this objection to homeschooling in the homeschooling literature, the objection is an extremely common one. Of course,

113

numerous homeschooled kids are well-adjusted, and many non-homeschooled kids have been scrambled by their "socialization."

Nevertheless, significant problems *are* relatively common among homeschooled children. One is the problem of children who crawl into the ground when someone says hello to them. Shyness is actually a form of rudeness, and lack of social confidence is common enough to note. The Bible says to "be courteous" (1 Pet. 3:8).

An opposite problem, overconfidence, can also develop. This might occur when a junior high student thinks he is in graduate school. For example, an only child who is homeschooled is always at the top of his class, and he can develop an unwarranted belief that he could be at the top of *any* class. But the Bible teaches that a Christian is "not to think of himself more highly than he ought to think, but to think soberly, as God has dealt to each one a measure of faith" (Rom. 12:3).

Either-Or Thinking. Homeschooling parents should also beware of thinking in either-or categories. For example, too often parents will say that they are emphasizing character over study and academics. But academics *is* a character issue. "How long will you slumber, O sluggard? When will you rise from your sleep?" (Prov. 6:9).

If we are forced to choose between godliness or learning, of course we must choose godliness. But who is making us submit to a choice like this? In our situation, we do not need to separate these elements of learning. Rather, as Christians who are involved in the task of education, we should see that to excel in the pursuit of learning is the pursuit of godliness.

Matriarchalism. And lastly, a final concern is that homeschooling too frequently tends to become matriarchal. Homeschooling must not be something a man "lets" his wife do. Recall that in Ephesians 6:4, Paul writes to fathers and says, "And you, fathers, . . . bring them up in the training and admonition of the Lord."

Many fathers make good Pharisees, binding heavy burdens on their wives, then not lifting a finger to help bear them.

Homeschooling cannot be what God intends for Christian education to be unless fathers are at the center of it. For example, they can help make decisions regarding curriculum, teach various classes, review work done during the day, encourage the entire family, identify problems before they arise, and ensure that godly discipline pervades the home.

Full Circle

And so we come full circle in our discussion of Christian education. Deuteronomy 6 does not just require that parents "see to it" that their children receive a Christian education. The word God places on us here includes not only the requirement that we talk of God's commandments, but that we talk of them in particular places. The places mentioned are "in your house," "when you travel as a family," "when you lie down," and "when you rise up."

While the responsibility we are given in Deuteronomy 6 does not directly name the use of a Christian school, it certainly requires that the Christian education received by our children include *every aspect of home life*—indeed, every aspect of life. In this sense, all Christian parents are required to be "homeschoolers." Christian parents who care for the education of their children must heed the warnings. We must all remember that God *will* strengthen us to do what He requires of us.

Christianity is a practical faith. The world works the way God intended it to work. But when we rebel against God and his design for the family, we doom ourselves to failure. It should come as no surprise, then, that government schools fail in many ways, and it is to this topic that we now turn.

15
CAN DO

*"I do not seek to understand in order that I may believe,
but I believe in order that I may understand."*
—ANSELM

For many historical and cultural reasons, Americans have a "can-do" mentality. Make it happen; make it work. We like the attitude of the Seebees, the Navy's Construction Battalion (CB) in the Second World War: "The difficult we can do right away; the impossible takes a little longer."

This attitude excites our admiration so much that sometimes we refuse to believe that we can't do what we can't do. Consequently, the only thing capable of bringing Americans up short on the question of government education is that, looking at the facts objectively, those schools are lousy. They are allowed to be immoral, ugly, and relativistic, yet as kids graduate without knowing how to read, everyone is up in arms. Why aren't parents more concerned about the effects of immorality, lack of beauty, and relativism?

Unworkable Pragmatism

Baal worship (fertility worship) was brought into northern Israel by Jezebel to make Israel lush and green. For those who worship the god of fertility, the point is to encourage fertility and growth. But after the people began to worship Baal, the living God saw to it through His prophet Elijah that it did not rain for three years. Worship the god of green, and, if that god is an idol, everything turns brown. ⁓

This is what has happened to us. Our idol as Americans has been pragmatism, and the only real problem with the god of "making it work" is that he cannot make it work. The god of seeing has no eyes; the god of hearing, no ears. The great god pragmatism has no hands.

The difficulties in our school system are well known. For example, literacy is not guaranteed. How is it possible for the president of the United States to call for a literacy program to ensure that all our children learn to read by third grade? We currently have compulsory education laws, everyone goes to school nine months a year—from K through 12, five days a week, eight hours a day. And we need a *literacy* program? Some of us apparently made a mistake when we thought the *schools* were supposed to be a literacy program.

Out of Control

Why don't government schools work? One reason is that discipline is required to make a school function. But discipline cannot really be separated from the concept of discipleship. And discipleship cannot be separated from service to Christ.

When students are taught that they are to live for themselves, we find it difficult to continue educating them when they start doing just that. Discipline and the kind of self-denial that is essential to a rigorous education are impossible for the general populace apart from the Christian faith. The great error of religious liberalism was the thought that ethical self-restraint could be detached from doctrinal commitments. As we should all be able to see by now, this enterprise does not work at all. True discipline will not return to classrooms until the Lord Jesus Christ returns to those classrooms.

Ol' Time Religion

Further, the acquisition of literacy requires a religious motive. When that religious motive declines, literacy declines. No one is going to bust a gut to make sure a child has lifelong access to the *National Enquirer* or Danielle Steele novels. But Christian parents have a moral and religious obligation to provide their children with access to the Word of God. That religious motive is as important as the salvation of their children.

– Another reason our schools are failing is that they do not seek God's blessing. Because they overtly reject the need to seek His blessing, they cannot be surprised when they do not receive it. The universe is not an impersonal place to live. God is always in the room and in the classroom. The question is whether we acknowledge His presence and authority. When we don't, we have no reason to suppose that He will shower the ungrateful with educational success.

Economics 101

And then, of course, we have the question of economic incentives. In some ways, the economic question really undergirds all this—not because economics is primary, but because on certain questions, the economic issues reveal an attempt to circumvent the authorities that God has established to handle the process of education.

If the family is the ministry of health, education, and welfare (and it is), then the family is equipped to accomplish what God has assigned. If parents pay a school to educate their children, then they have the authority of a customer and can demand accountability. But if taxpayers pay into a vast pot, they are not really buying any service in particular. This means that government schools are inefficient for the same reason that the post office is not as efficient as UPS. Government schools have no bottom line that they can analyze and correlate with what they accomplish in the classroom.

Because parents are getting the education for "free," they do not have economic standing to complain about the "service" they receive for their money. Ultimately, they don't really receive *anything* for their money. Their money is taken from them regardless of whether they have any kids. In short, government education is socialism applied to education, and the only astonishing thing is why so many conservatives who want to save "our" government schools do not recognize that they are, in fact, functionally socialistic.

The Greatest of These . . .

Another reason why government education does not work is that it does not present knowledge as something to be pursued out of love. The state is necessarily coercive. As George Washington pointed out so astutely, the state does not rest upon persuasion, but rather upon force. If we begin coercing people in various directions apart from God's permission to do so, we cannot be surprised when we eventually provoke resentment and lack of cooperation.

Compulsory education is oxymoronic. It is the inevitable end produced by the god of pragmatism—the idea that we can educate everyone if we merely put enough legal strength into our efforts. When we consider what we should be willing to *force* other people to do, the answer should be limited to those things God requires us to force upon them. For example, we should be willing to force people to refrain from murder, stealing, adultery, and so forth. But we should not force them to quit smoking, eating refined sugar, coveting, lusting, and engaging in other similar activities. Neither should the state try to force people out of their ignorance with compulsory education.

Sins and Crimes

This leads us to the distinction between *sins* and *crimes*. A crime is a particular behavior which has a civil penalty attached to it. A sin is something which is morally reprehensible but which should not have a civil penalty attached to it. Assuming just laws, all crimes are sins, but not all sins should be crimes. Lazy ignorance is certainly a sin, but ought not be a crime. Consequently, compulsory education should appall us because it is a sin that has been elevated to a crime.

Because we have blurred the distinction between sins and crimes and have penalized people for their sins, at the end of the day, the busy statist will be manufacturing sin-laws to penalize sinners.

Back to the school system. We have required all taxpayers to pay for a school system they may or may not use. This requirement has the force of a penalty, making it a crime not to use the system. This is more than just theoretical for many Christian parents around the country who have school-aged children they did not enroll at the local government school. What is their crime? Connect this to compulsory education laws, and you have quite a tyranny going.

The solution is to suffer quietly and pay the price for two systems of education. This is God's penalty, imposed on us for what we did to others when we controlled the school system. If we receive the discipline quietly with appropriate confession of sin, God may be merciful. And as we reflect on how far we have drifted from God's pattern of education, we should come to learn that idols never do what they promise. The gods of pragmatism have certainly failed us, and we need to return to the God of our fathers.

We must go back, then, to the fact that true Christian education always takes place in a covenantal context. Out of this covenant true wisdom flows. In the next chapter, we will explore this covenantal context.

16
THE COVENANTAL CONTEXT

✴ "There is not a square inch of ground in heaven or on earth or under the earth in which there is peace between Christ and Satan . . . If you say that you are 'not involved' you are involved in Satan's side. If you say you are involved in the struggle . . . in the area of the family and in the church, but not in the school, you are deceiving yourself." ✴
—ROUSAS J. RUSHDOONY

Children are born into a covenant relationship with their parents. Of course, this relationship is supposed to grow and mature over time, but whether it does or not, the covenant establishes the relationship at the beginning.

When growth and maturity are missing, the reason can always be attributed to sin. Whenever sin gets tangled up in any covenant relationship, its effect is always destructive. Clearly, when such sins as bitterness, resentment, and rebellion are involved, the destruction in the relationship is obvious. At the end of the process, parents and children find themselves unable to speak to one another, and everyone sees the problem.

Legalism Then and Now

Another kind of sin is less obvious in its destructive effects. This sin can destroy relationships where everything appears to be well-ordered and everyone believes that all is fine. When this problem is present, a child can appear to be doing very well in a government school (they are one of the "good" kids), so the parents assume that everything is fine. Detaching authority from persons and generating a disembodied set of rules are common errors and at times hard to see.

This was the error of the Pharisees who studied the Scriptures because they thought that in those Scriptures—detached from the One who gave the Scriptures—they would find eternal life. Jesus rebuked this folly and said that the Scriptures bore witness to Him (John 5:39–40). This same error was embraced by all the unbelievers in the Old Testament who, for some reason, could not see Christ in the Law (Rom. 10:3–4).

The same thing happens on a smaller scale in the home. When one of the parents says to do something, this frequently does not carry as much weight as a list of rules written up and posted on the fridge. A certain kind of mind likes abstract law. When the law comes from "nowhere," i.e., written rules, the person following the rule can be very scrupulous and tidy-minded about obeying it, and yet not really be obeying anyone but himself—certainly not obeying the person who made the rules, the parent. This is veneered obedience "with the look of real wood"!

Certain personalities like things in straight little rows. When such a personality is born into a home, life will be more pleasant later on, at least in some respects. The parent who does not have to constantly get after a child to make his bed or pick up his shoes has fewer daily tasks to hassle with. But this behavior on the part of the child is not necessarily true obedience; it may sometimes be as willful and stubborn as outright defiance or rebellion. Outward obedience can be passive rebellion. True obedience is a matter of the heart.

Sometimes children impose this covert rebellion on the workings of the home, sometimes the parents teach it, and other times the two work together in tandem to produce a bad problem.

Covenantal Love

This problem is often what lies behind certain forms of compulsive behavior in children. Compulsive behavior can be understood as submission to an arbitrary and sometimes irrational standard detached from the requirements of the parents who love the child and detached from the Word of a personal God. Love is not only the fulfillment of the law; love is the ballast of the law. Without love (i.e., without relationship in covenant), any Herculean achievements amount to nothing.

The thing accomplished through compulsive behavior might be impressive, but Paul dismisses it as worthless anyway. "Though I bestow all my goods to feed the poor, and though I give my body to be burned, but have not love, it profits me nothing" (1 Cor. 13:3). We tend to read this passage with the meaning that great accomplishments are worthless in the presence of malice, spite, resentment, hatred, and all the rest. But great deeds are also worthless when done in the *absence* of love. The man who feeds the poor may have nothing against them, but his effort is still worthless because it was conducted in an abstracted realm of rules, regulations, duties, and obligations, not obedience out of love. This abstract obedience is a constant temptation for "good" children.

When parents discipline in the personal way that they ought to, the obedience they receive is cheerful because it proceeds from personal loyalty. When parents allow the discipline to become something abstract and detached from covenant (detached from a relationship of love), obedience becomes something hung from an invisible skyhook. A man may grow up in a strict home and live that way himself, yet not have any loyalty to his father. Because things were strict, there was *conformity* but no *loyalty*. But true obedience proceeds from personal loyalty.

Therefore, the rules in a Christian home should be basic and should always be related directly to the relationships God placed at the center of the home. My son suggested this entire line of thought to me after observing it in a family we knew. In this family, all the rules of the household plainly and obviously reduced to one: *Obey your father*. The children delighted in doing so. Just as a believer cannot look at the law without seeing Christ, so a child should not be able to look at a requirement of the household without seeing his father. The law and the man should blur together. And this is love.

Too Late

When we consider this truth, as well as other aspects of childrearing, we would do well to meditate on the words "too late."

Once children grow up and are matured, the work of childrearing is all done. Parents therefore have what might be called a fleeting opportunity as they bring up their children. This two-year-old will be two years old once, and this teenager will only be a teenager once. In later years, when parents have much more time for reflection, those seasons of opportunity will seem like a moment. Many lessons God requires us to instill during those times cannot be instilled later.

But before that moment is past and before the consequences of unwise parental care become evident, the approaching problems are frequently ignored by some parents in the name of a particular theory or notion. Many such parents have a tight grip on a theory that they have been told will cover them. And it certainly does seem to cover them—until it is too late and the damage is done. If a parent assumes that literacy is best acquired when a child is twelve and waits until then, the results will not be pretty.

Covenant Community

Childrearing occurs in the context of a covenant community. In the same way, baptism should not occur in a private ceremony. It should be done in the presence of God's people who, together with the Lord, witness the vows being made. This means that within certain limits how your child is doing is the business of others as well as your own. They have a responsibility to pray for you and your children, and, when appropriate, to say something to you about how your kids are doing.

But parents are often prickly when it comes to any kind of criticism, express or implied, with regard to their dear ones. This is a natural temptation; it comes with the flesh. When told that your child was a premier stinker at that birthday party, the flesh wants to locate the problem anywhere outside your kid. "They obviously weren't being supervised properly." At the end of the day, the excuses which parents make, and which they teach their children to make, can often be simply absurd. When informed that a sullen teenager is down at the corner giving the finger to passing motorists, Mother may rush to fit this news into the categories she has already established for herself. "He is still struggling with his shyness. He is trying to come out of his shell."

Parental Defensiveness

—We must resist as sin defensiveness against criticism coming from the covenant community. In resisting, we are doing what every godly parent in the history of the world has had to do at some time. But in the modern world, family and childrearing fads and fashions come and go, bringing with them a peculiar kind of defensiveness. When such childrearing fashions arise in the Christian world, they present themselves as a lost-but-now-recovered bit of biblical wisdom, a wisdom which our modern age has, of course, overlooked. The temptation to think this way is compelling to many because modernity has lost or rejected many aspects of biblical wisdom.

–Sin is hard enough to resist at any time, but the worst danger comes when we are sinning in the name of righteousness and wisdom. We reason that since biblical wisdom looks strange to secular modernists, anything that looks strange to them must be biblical wisdom. Therefore, greater prickliness or defensiveness comes from those who are in the grip of a theory claiming to be wisdom. Those who really have recovered an element of biblical wisdom are not defensive over it. Godly parents know that some of their practices look like a basket of fruit to the modernists, and the fact that modernists misunderstand is good for a laugh around the dinner table. But prickliness is often a defense for the indefensible.

For example, the Bible contains clear and overt teaching on the subject of child discipline, so when a concerned brother warns a parent about lax discipline, he has a plain biblical case. But suppose that the problem is more obtuse because the parent has read a book by an education expert who believes that sons shouldn't be taught to read until they feel like it. The son is now thirteen and doesn't feel like it yet. The problem is more difficult to pin down, and when the issue eventually does become clear, the concrete is dry and the son is illiterate. When the parent is approached before the consequences are apparent, he can feel like his brother is overstepping his bounds and meddling on the basis of a mere difference in educational theory. If he is approached after the damage is done, then what we have is another barn door, another horse.

I have seen multiple examples of this kind of thing. When parental openness to outside input finally comes and the faults in the various theories are finally acknowledged, it is too late to do anything about it. Sometimes this happens because the "theory" was bogus. Sometimes it happens when the theory was good, but the practice fell far short of the theory, and if anyone asked about the practice, the theory was immediately defended. It is not hard to lead those who seek an escape from accountability on a merry chase.

One theory says that no one knows your child better than you do. It would be more accurate to say that no one is in a better position to know their child than the parents, provided the parents conduct themselves with wisdom. If they do not, the chances are good that everyone in the church will know the character of the child better than the parents do.

Parental wisdom is not automatic. Parental defensiveness is. And harvest is a bad time to decide that you don't like what you planted in your child.

True Parental Wisdom

Wisdom is not made out of wood and neither are our children. When Christian parents seek to bring together wisdom and children, they must resist all wooden techniques. They must be wise themselves, and wisdom is supple. The only useful wood in the whole scenario is that of the spanking paddle, provided it is not applied by parents with wooden heads.

> My son, if you receive my words, and treasure my commands within you, so that you incline your ear to wisdom, and apply your heart to understanding; yes, if you cry out for discernment, and lift up your voice for understanding, if you seek her as silver, and search for her as for hidden treasures; then you will understand the fear of the LORD, and find the knowledge of God.

For the LORD gives wisdom; from His mouth come knowledge and understanding (Prov. 2:1–6).

Consider the verbs a concerned father uses to urge his son in this instruction: receive, treasure, incline, apply, cry out, lift up, seek, search, understand, and find. In our modern approach to child-rearing, we want one verb equipped with an on/off switch—do and don't.

Because we want our children to "do" and "not do," we look for books and instruction that will teach us how to be parents the same way. Do this and don't do that. Okay, we say, and perform our assigned task, whatever it was, and then like a dog that just returned with the stick, we sit expectantly waiting for our next assignment. We have connected all the dots, painted all the numbers, fetched all the sticks, and attended all the workshops. Now we only have to wait on the promises of God!

But the wisdom required for parenting is not well represented by a single on/off switch. A better picture would be fifty-eight switches for each kid—all of them equipped with a dimmer attachment. Parenting is hard work, and the hardest part is the pursuit of wisdom.

We tend to assume that this hard work of parenting means nothing more than parents getting up in the middle of the night, working hard to provide for physical needs, and diligently disciplining. Of course, they need to do these things, but the center of our labors is pursuing wisdom—study, meditation, prayer, and obedience—in which our children are included. ("Oh, good! He listed four things to do!")

All this may create a temptation to despair. How is it possible for us to do this? We are sinful and fallen, and we think the task is way beyond us. Can anyone be wise? We can follow a checklist; so, we tell the experts, give us that checklist! We want our instructors to provide us with a Jiffy Lube for the soul. So how, then, do we find wisdom?

Pursue Wisdom

First, the Bible instructs us to *pursue* wisdom. Scripture tells us that this is both difficult and possible. Mining gold is possible, but not in your back yard. You must travel to the mine. A man can feed himself, but not by lying on his back with his mouth open.

When Scripture tells us to pursue wisdom in how we bring up our children, we must always remember that these words are given to us in *our* condition. Proverbs, for example, was not given to the angels Gabriel and Michael, who don't have any kids. This means that when we urge our sons to search for wisdom as for hidden treasure, we must know from experience as forgiven sinners what that search is like. It is not like playing hide-and-seek with a two-year-old.

We have become so lazy that the complexities associated with the pursuit of wisdom are written off as impossible or are confused with relativism. Suppose one of our children has been caught doing something that is clearly sinful. We want someone to tell us what we are supposed to do about it. If the response is "it depends," we think we are dealing with creeping liberalism. Now relativists will certainly say that everything depends, but so will wise men who are well-versed in God's absolutes. So how can we tell them apart? It depends.

From the Lord

Second, we must consider the conclusion of Proverbs 2:1–6. The Lord gives wisdom, and from His mouth come knowledge and understanding. When we pursue, treasure, or seek "wisdom" from any storehouse other than that which He has given, we will be frustrated over and over again.

Wisdom is based squarely upon the grace of God. He gives it. When He does not give it, it is not there. The search for wisdom, therefore, is both relational and propositional. We must know the One who speaks and what He has said.

Wisdom comes only from the Lord. Psalm 111:10 tells us that wisdom begins with the fear of the Lord. Christian parents, first and foremost, must seek His wisdom. This search does not always reside in everyone who speaks in His name.

Christian schools are no panacea. Nothing good is automatic in a fallen world. The only thing my garden can grow automatically is weeds.

Therefore, unless children are taught in a Christian school by teachers who have wisdom, unless they are put there by parents acting in wisdom, unless children are being taught to love the Lord their God in all wisdom, then the educational endeavor is fruitless. Put bluntly, some people can do wrong while they are doing right. Parents who *presume* are parents who place their children in spiritual danger no matter where their children attend school.

But for those parents who come to the Lord in truth, studying His Word, seeking His wisdom, acting in faith, the promises are wonderful. Your children will rise and call you blessed.

This brings us to see Christ as our all in all in every endeavor, especially concerning the education of our children.

17
OUR ALL
IN ALL

"Every student shall consider the main end of his study to wit to know God in Jesus Christ and answerably to lead a Godly, sober life."
—FOUNDERS OF YALE COLLEGE

Because the state is the great idol of modernity, Christians have to think through what things are lawful to render to Caesar and what things are not. We must soberly consider the nature of our problem—the corruption of the system and the corruption of those Christians who continue to have their children educated in government schools.

We do not view our current state of affairs or take action as rebels; we must also remember the civil *submission* required of us in the Bible. This submission does *not* include submitting our children, and so, any call for social transformation must begin where we have begun—within the household of God.

Disintegrating Culture

As we look around at our disintegrating culture, the cry of Psalm 94 is on our lips:

> O LORD God, to whom vengeance belongs; O God, to whom vengeance belongs, shine forth! Rise up, O Judge of the earth; render punishment to the proud. LORD, how long will the wicked, how long will the wicked triumph? . . . Shall the throne of iniquity, which devises evil by law, have fellowship with You? They gather

together against the life of the righteous, and condemn innocent blood (Ps. 94:1–3,20–21).

The Bible recognizes what we might call *de facto* rule. The ones in power are put there by God. But the Bible also teaches the concept of *moral legitimacy*. "It is an abomination for kings to commit wickedness, for a throne is established by righteousness" (Prov. 16:12; see also Prov. 20:28; 25:5; 29:14). So where do we as a people stand?

Since *Roe v. Wade*, we as a nation have maintained that the dismemberment of an infant in the womb is morally legitimate. But the Bible says that murder is evil and *defiles a land* (Exod. 20:13; Num. 35:33–34), and that the unborn in a just society are to have full legal protection (Exod. 21:22–25). Christian parents who have their kids in government schools want their children educated by the same people who brought us this bloodbath, and who *defend* the monstrosity in these schools.

In our culture, moral filth is exalted. From pornographic and federally funded "art," to twisted sex education courses, to homosexual marriages, to vile behavior in the White House, our culture defies God (Rom. 1:28–32). Consistent Christians will defy this culture. But many of our number have not yet made the break. They want their children to be taught morality by those who are self-evidently clueless concerning the nature of true morality.

A Nation of Fools

Our nation hates the truth. From the central lie of our government school system that the living God is irrelevant, to the dishonest ways in which we handle the law, we have turned away from truth. The prophet Jeremiah proclaims:

> How can you say, "We are wise, and the law of the LORD is with us?" Look, the false pen of the scribe certainly works falsehood. The wise men are ashamed, they are dismayed and taken. Behold, they have rejected the word of the LORD; so what wisdom do they have? (Jer. 8:8–9).

What wisdom do they have? None, the Bible says. But we say they must have enough wisdom to teach *our* kids.

Our culture is afflicted with bogus crusades. Because we will not learn our morality from the law of God, we find ourselves inventing our own lists of things to be indignant about, including tobacco, rain forests, and western European history. Christian parents nonetheless still enroll their children to be taught by these crusaders who have just enough wisdom to make a jaybird fly crooked.

In summary, our modern educators cannot be dismayed at those Christians who deny that modern educators have moral legitimacy because modern educators want to insist that in the final analysis, there is no such thing as moral legitimacy. As followers of the Word of God, we can have only one thing to say to such wickedness in high places (Isa. 5:20–21). But we cannot speak this way if our children are still there.

The Log in Our Eye

It would be wonderful to be able to say that the corruption in our centers of power has nothing to do with us, but God gives rulers in order to chastise a people. "Righteousness exalts a nation, but sin is a reproach to any people" (Prov. 14:34). Our government schools are established to propagate sin. This is why these schools are a reproach to us and will continue to be as long as our children are there.

And consider the state of the church. How do we expect civil rulers to conduct their affairs according to the Word of God when the *church* won't do so? We have lost our saltiness as outlined in Matthew 5:13–16, so we send our children to government schools where they are trampled on by men.

We cannot effectively resist corruption because we still serve the idol of personal comfort. Why do we yell when they want us to pay for the privileges we greedily accept? "I spoke to you in your prosperity, but you said, 'I will not hear.' This has been your manner from your youth, that you did not obey My voice" (Jer. 22:21). If you hear the word of righteousness when you are *not* afflicted, you do well. How many Christian parents took their children out of government schools in the days of our prosperity? Not many.

Because we have not prepared for this battle, when we are finally provoked to action, our prior sloth will result in foolish and ill-considered action. The school of resistance to lawless thrones is the same as the school of submission to the lordship of Christ within the church. This school is not a three-week course, but rather a lifelong endeavor. Having our children educated by the enemy is not a good way to start.

We serve the living God, the Holy One of Israel. He never changes; His attitude toward sinful nations is always the same. His wrath is visited upon all who defy Him, those who walk along spitting at the very clouds. The only way to flee *from* God is to flee to God. The only way to flee *to* God is through His Christ, our Lord Jesus. Christian parents have no business turning back to Him without bringing their children with them.

Faith and Good Works

When we consider what we as parents should act like, what first comes to mind? Our tendency is to rush to a works orientation, rather than resting in faith. But the gospel always calls us to *faith*.

> I am not ashamed of the gospel of Christ, for it is the power of God to salvation for everyone who believes, for the Jew first and also for the Greek. For in it the righteousness of God is revealed *from faith to faith*; as it is written, "The just shall live by faith" (Rom. 1:16–17).

God does not call us to exhibit this faith in every area of life *except* childrearing. This faith is to be exhibited in all of life, *especially* in childrearing, since God promises to be our God and the God of our children after us from generation to generation: "Therefore know that the LORD your God, He is God, the faithful God who keeps covenant and mercy *for a thousand generations* with those who love Him and keep His commandments" (Deut. 7:9).

All things, especially the work of educating our children, should be governed by faith, and faith alone. "Then they said to

Him, 'What shall we do, that we may work the works of God?' Jesus answered and said to them, '*This is the work of God, that you believe* in Him whom He sent'" (John 6:28–29).

Godly parents are characterized by their faith, which means that they are confident, trusting, quiet, serene. Of course, godly parents exhibit good works, but such works are the fruit of their faith. Their works exceed the righteousness of the Pharisees, but they would not dream of trusting in those works. The heart of godly parenting is faith—faith from beginning to end.

From Faith to Faith

The human race is divided into two categories: *covenant-keepers* and *covenant-breakers*. When we make this division, we immediately tend to assume that covenant keepers do so on the basis of *their works*. But the covenant is kept in only one way—by faith, from first to last. Trusting in our works is how we *break* covenant. In the covenant of grace, God has been kind enough to promise us our children. We do not appropriate this promise through what *we* might do, but through faith. And when we appropriate it by faith, that will affect what we do.

Covenant blessings are promised us; God gives the promise to a thousand generations to those who keep His covenant. So what do we do to keep His covenant? What good things can we do? This brings us back to the words of Christ in John 6:29: "This is the work of God, that you *believe*." The believing about which Christ speaks is firm and constant; the trust and belief we exhibit toward God is not a sporadic or momentary thing. This is what we see in Romans 1—our lives are lived from faith to faith.

Where does this faith arise? The Bible teaches that faith comes from hearing the Word of God. If the Holy Spirit gives you ears to hear that Word, you will hear it. And what are we to believe? We are to believe the Word of God, all of it, and with regard to educating our children, we are to trust God at His Word with regard to our children and their children after them.

When are we to believe? As with other aspects of our lives, time and history matter. We cannot believe God's promises for the salvation of a child if that child has already died in rebellion. This is another way of saying that there is a time of opportunity and such a thing as *too late*. If a child is grown up and in rebellion because of his upbringing, God may still show grace and mercy. We should pray for Him to do so. But this grace would be in spite of the way the child was raised, not in fulfillment of the covenant promises to covenant parents, who, by His grace, exhibited faithfulness in their parenting.

Means and Ends

The question of God's sovereignty still nags at us. To answer it, we must recall the doctrine of means and ends. God never ordains anything willy-nilly. A good order and purpose attends all that He does. We understand the principle if we consider the subject of evangelism: God is the final cause of everything, but He ordains the use of instrumental (secondary) causes to accomplish His purposes, such as the preaching of the gospel. We should simply apply this to our children. Trusting God to keep His Word does not contradict His sovereignty. How could it?

We worship a sovereign God who uses means to accomplish His ends. Parents are the means to educate and train their children in the nurture and admonition of the Lord. He promises to be our all in all every step along the way. We always need to remember two truths. First, we are not sufficient for these things. And second, He is our sufficiency. What He demands of us in the Law, He graciously gives us in the gospel.

May we praise Him all the days of our lives as we educate and train our children to join us around His glorious throne!